# VOICES OF FAITH

## The Women Who Shaped Scripture

## Chris Dunn

**Divine Insights Publications**

Divine Insights
PUBLICATIONS

ISBN: 979-8-89965-257-8

Cover design by: Divine Insights Publications
Printed in the United Kingdom

# CONTENTS

# WOMEN IN THE BIBLE: THE FACTS

Certain research found that a survey of the Bible resulted in the discovery of between 3000 and 3100 different names. From the total, 170 were female individuals out of this number. The findings, however, showed a total of 1700 unique personal names in the Bible after they had eliminated any potential duplicates from the results. Women, in total, there are 137 of them.

These biblical women encompass a variety of locations and generations, beginning with Miriam, the sister of Moses, in the Old Testament and continuing with Mary Magdalene in the New Testament. Even though we do not have information pertaining to each one of these women, their lives present us with lessons that are valuable for us today.

In the Bible, who was the first lady to be mentioned?

Eve is the first woman mentioned in the Bible. She was fashioned by God from the rib of Adam, the first man, with the intention of being his partner and assistant in the Garden of Eden. Eve, as the mother of all living things, was a significant figure in the human narrative and in the realization of God's divine purpose through the ages.

In the Bible, how many females are there?

In the Bible, there are more than 170 ladies who are mentioned, each of whom has a different story and makes a different contribution to the tale of God's people. In addition to being faithful followers, these women have served as leaders, prophets, and mothers, inspiring countless generations with their courage and devotion to their faith.

Who was the very first female to preach in the Bible?

Deborah, a prophetess and judge of Israel, is commonly acknowledged as the first woman to ever preach according to the teachings of the Bible. In addition to leading the Israelites to victory in battle, her tale is a tribute to the strength that women can possess in spiritual and leadership positions.

In which part of the Bible is the virtuous woman mentioned?

The Bible provides a description of a virtuous woman in Proverbs 31. This chapter, which is commonly referred to as the "Proverbs 31 woman," identifies the traits and qualities of an ideal woman, with particular emphasis on her intelligence, hard work, compassion, and reverence for God.

In the Bible, who is the most senior lady?

In the Bible, the oldest woman is not stated explicitly by age demographic. When she gave birth to their son Isaac, however, Sarah, who was married to Abraham, is well-known for her old age at the time of his delivery. When she became pregnant with Isaac, she was ninety years old, making her one of the oldest women that is referenced in the Bible.

# FOREWORD

Even though women have attained remarkable accomplishments within the context of the religious tradition, their voices have frequently been disregarded in the texts of the Bible. This is a terrible state of affairs. This article is intended to analyse the major contributions that women have made to the formation of biblical scripture, as well as the repercussions that these contributions have had on religious belief and theology.

We can gain a more in-depth understanding of the tremendous impact that these women had on the theological controversies and biblical stories that they were involved in through the performance of an analysis pertaining to the roles that women such as Miriam, Deborah, and Mary Magdalene performed.

In our own lives, we can find a consistent source of inspiration by drawing inspiration from the lives of several women who are mentioned in the Bible. From handmaidens to powerful queens, these ladies portray a diverse spectrum of characters across the board.

On the other hand, these twenty extraordinary ladies from the scriptures are certain to have a profound and long-lasting impact on you, although you may or may not be in search of courage and strength or faithfulness and devotion. They not only serve as a wonderful example of what it means to completely embrace one's purpose in life, but they also serve as a magnificent example of what it means to be obedient to God.

From Miriam, the sister of Moses in the Old Testament to Mary Magdalene in the New Testament, these biblical women cover a broad range of ages and regions. Although we do not have information on every one of these women, their lives provide us with lessons that are applicable to the present time. Let's take a comprehensive look at the stories of the nineteen extraordinary ladies who are mentioned in the Bible.

As demonstrated by the Old Testament, there are an incredible number of wonderful women who lived in the past and who were influential leaders in the history of God's people. These women have had a profound and everlasting influence on the narrative that is presented in the Bible, beginning with Eve, the first woman, and continuing with courageous leaders such as Deborah and Esther. During their journey through difficult times, they exhibited wisdom, faith, and tenacity, and in many instances, they challenged the standards and expectations of society.

Not only do we get the chance to learn important lessons from the stories of these ten extraordinary women from the Old Testament as we investigate their lives, but we also get the opportunity to appreciate the strength and beauty that is inherent in their steadfast faith and dedication to God.

The New Testament presents us with a number of exceptional ladies who have made significant contributions to the tale of God's people. These ladies come from a diverse range of extraordinary women. These women have shown courage, devotion, and spiritual insight throughout their journeys with God. They include the humble and obedient Mary, who was the mother of Jesus, as well as the loyal Mary Magdalene, who was also devoted to God. While we are looking into the lives of these ten remarkable women from the New Testament, let us take lessons from their examples and acknowledge the tremendous impact that they have had on the development of the Gospel and the establishment of the early Christian church.

As a result of their uncompromising devotion to Christ and their willingness to minister to others, these women have left a legacy on the Christian religion and continue to serve as examples for future generations.

# PART 1: WOMEN IN THE OLD TESTAMENT: STRENGTH, WISDOM, AND FAITH

Not only does the Old Testament provide a wealth of stories that narrate the history of God's people, but it also brings to light the outstanding achievements of women who were instrumental in shaping that history. These women exemplify strength, intelligence, and faith in the face of difficulty. They range from Eve, the first woman, whose decisions laid the foundation for the beginning of humanity, to the strong and wise leaders such as Deborah and the brave queen Esther. Their narratives are interwoven with the tapestry of biblical history, which serves as an example of how they coped with difficult challenges with bravery and resilience, frequently challenging the norms and expectations of society.

Through this exploration of ten extraordinary women from the Old Testament, we will dig into the unique journeys that each of them went through and the teachings that they impart. Each of these women went through their own set of difficulties and challenges, but they were able to emerge as strong leaders whose legacies continue to serve as a source of inspiration thanks to their unshakable faith and dedication to God. In the process of reflecting on their lives, we will discover the deep strength and beauty that lies hidden inside their tales. This discovery will inspire us to accept our own faith and tenacity in our current day-to-day lives.

As we begin this journey through the pages of the Old Testament, we invite you to join us in celebrating the everlasting impact that these women have had on the biblical story and uncovering the enduring values that continue to resonate with us in the present day. Their narratives serve as a reminder that faith is not something that should be held passively; rather, it is an active force that has the potential to bring about transformation, empowerment, and a greater comprehension of God's purpose for our lives.

# THE ROLE OF EVE IN THE GENESIS NARRATIVE

The Lord God said, "It is not good for the man to be alone.
I will make a helper suitable for him." (Genesis 1:18)

According to the Book of Genesis, Eve is depicted as the first woman, who was created by God from the rib of Adam to be his partner. She is a key player in the story that revolves around the Garden of Eden, which makes her role very important. This chapter will investigate the significance of Eve's creation and the decisions she made, demonstrating how these choices relate to the themes of free connection and free will, and ultimately leading to an understanding of the sin and suffering that exist in the world. Eve's actions not only have an impact on her own story, but they also lay the framework for the moral and ethical challenges that humanity will face, which are echoed throughout the teachings of the Bible.

In the book of Genesis, it is stated that God created Eve to be Adam's eternal partner. She was brought into this world with the purpose of alleviating Adam's loneliness and creating a oneness that reflects the perfection of the divine. The creation of this fundamental entity marks the beginning of interpersonal relationships and lays the groundwork for life in the community. According to the New Revised Standard Version of Genesis 2:18 (NSRV), "It is not good that the man should be alone; I will make him a helper fit for him." Not only has this relationship been understood as a marital one, but it has also been viewed as a representation of the interconnectedness of humans.

This condition of innocence was quickly disrupted by what theologians and academics have come to refer to as 'The Fall.' The deception of Eve by the serpent, as described in Genesis 3, is an event that has piqued the interest of scholars, particularly in relation to the theological and ethical implications of the incident. The narrative experiences a significant shift when Eve consumes the fruit of the Tree of Knowledge of Good and Evil and gives it to Adam, who is also known as the first man. As a result of this deed, the couple's eyes are opened to good and evil, and they become aware of their nakedness, which is a symbol for the loss of innocence and the emergence of feelings of shame and guilt.

In the past, Eve has served as a symbol for both the innate curiosity and wants that are a part of human nature.

Augustine of Hippo and other early Christian authors provided interpretations that centred on original sin and the functions of genders in the context of their writings. According to Augustine's view of theology, the original sin was believed to have an impact on all of humanity. This perspective underscores the transition from a condition of grace to one that is tainted by sin and death (Brown, 2013).

The role and significance of Eve have transcended far beyond the bounds of religious texts, having an impact on cultural and gender perspectives. The story of Eve was frequently used in medieval literature to illustrate women's supposed vulnerability to temptation, which served to reinforce patriarchal attitudes toward women. Despite this, more recent academic work has involved a re-examination of these narratives. The narrative of Eve is seen by contemporary feminist readings as a reflection of the historical marginalization of women. These readings have advocated for interpretations that portray Eve as a symbol of human agency and a challenge to oppressive social structures (Trible, 1978).

The narrative of Eve has ramifications that extend into the realm of theology. According to the notion of original sin, which is derived from this narrative, humanity is fundamentally broken and in need of redemption from the divine. Baptism is seen by the Catholic Church as a cleansing rite that removes original sin, according to the Catechism of the Catholic Church (2019). This idea has had a significant impact on doctrines such as Catholicism's view on baptism.

In addition, the ethical discourse on free will that is presented in Eve's story establishes a biblical precedent for the moral framework. The decision to consume the forbidden fruit can be analysed from the perspective of moral and ethical decision-making processes. The story highlights the tension that exists between human free will and divine authority. This discourse has a critically relevant impact on the ongoing debates in contemporary ethical and moral philosophy.

In the Western arts and letters, the Genesis narrative has become a fundamental archetype because of the extensive references that artists and authors have made to it throughout history. The 'Paradise Lost' by Milton is a classic work that addresses the Fall of man. It depicts Eve as not only the source of sin, but also as the person who started the redemptive story that ultimately led to Christ's sacrifice (Milton, 1667). Milton's portrayal of Eve's character emphasizes her intricacy by demonstrating her aspirations, anxieties, and the regrets she experiences in the end.

In the course of human history, the story of Eve has been utilized as a tool to both support and question the gender roles and standards that society adheres to. In numerous societies influenced by Christianity, interpretations of the narrative of Eve were used to educate and rationalize the oppression and discrimination of women. These interpretations frequently referred to the Genesis text that discusses Eve being deceived first (1 Timothy 2:14) as divine endorsement of male authority. The development of feminist theology, on the other hand, provides important re-readings of the Genesis texts, which challenges the established patriarchal interpretations of those texts.

In the opinions of modern scholars such as Phyllis Trible and Elizabeth Cady Stanton, Eve's deeds and character should be reinterpreted as being indicative of power and agency rather than passivity and mistake (Trible, 1992; Stanton, 1972). The significance of this reinterpretation lies in the broader movement it represents, which aims to remedy gender inequity and patriarchal prejudices in both the religious and secular spheres of society.

In addition to Christianity, the tale of Eve is of great importance in other Abrahamic religions, particularly Judaism and Islam. There are variances in interpretation of Eve's role in Judaism, with some viewing her as more of a partner and less of the person who started the sin.

When it comes to ecology, psychology, and the human condition, the figure of Eve is frequently referenced in contemporary discussions. Lynn White Jr.'s critique of Judeo-Christian stewardship for environmental degradation due to dominion theology is an example of how her tale has been utilized metaphorically to discuss the ecological impact that humanity has had. The narrative also acts as an allegory for comprehending human disobedience and the psychological origins of disobedience, according to its role in popular psychology.

As scholarly and societal perspectives continue to change, the story of Eve and the many ways it has been understood are being re-evaluated, which will very certainly result in further shifts across theological, cultural, and social environments. The upcoming research has the potential to continue unravelling the complex meanings of Eve's story, as well as the possibility of incorporating a wider range of cultural perspectives and scientific insights to inform theological reinterpretations.

The acceptance of feminist interpretations of Eve may be facilitated by the efforts of societies striving toward gender equality to continue contesting traditional readings of Eve that support patriarchal systems. In addition, environmental ethics may increasingly engage with the narrative of Eden, utilizing it as a literary device to meditate on humanity's relationship with the natural world.

The role that Eve played as the first woman, her creation, and the subsequent events that led to the Fall of Man serve to illustrate important components of human existence, such as innocence, temptation, sin, and redemption. Through the perspectives of history and culture, Eve has been interpreted in a variety of ways, and her narrative has proven to be a fruitful source for theological, ethical, and social conversations. Her story continues to have an impact on religious beliefs and cultural standards, and it serves as an enduring symbol of the theological significance and human complexity that are characteristic of her narrative. Even as interpretations change in response to contemporary values and academic research, the symbol of Eve is expected to continue being relevant, since it reflects the timeless concerns of morality, autonomy, and human identity in a variety of contexts that are both changing and evolving.

The creation of Eve from the rib of Adam is symbolic of the close bond that was meant to exist between men and women. This relationship is one of partnership rather than hierarchies (Genesis 2:22). Through the lens of Eden, where Adam and Eve live in harmony, tending to the garden and delighting in its blessings together, this concept of companionship is further developed and illustrated. Nevertheless, the moment that Eve has an interaction with the serpent is a critical juncture that marks a paradigm shift from companionship to individuality. At this point, she is confronted with a decision that will have a lasting impact on both her life and Adam's life together. This narrative makes use of the theme of companionship as a foundation for investigating human relationships and the underlying vulnerabilities that come with them. It shows that although companionship is a divine purpose, it also exposes individuals to moral dilemmas (Wright, 2010).

The seduction of Eve by the serpent is the event that brings free will, which is a vital component of the Genesis story, into the picture. Even though she was warned not to eat from the Tree of Knowledge of Good and Evil, Eve's decision to consume the fruit is a representation of the battle that exists between obedience and desire, according to Genesis 3:4-6. The act of disobedience that is being discussed is significant because it brings up questions regarding the essence of human freedom and responsibility. Even though Eve's decision was influenced by external temptation, it is ultimately a reflection of her agency. This suggests that true freedom includes the ability to make choices that have the potential to have repercussions. As a result of this act, sin was able to enter the world, which not only signalled the fall of humanity but also laid the groundwork for comprehending moral decision-making in relation to divine command (Wright, 2010).

The disobedience of Eve and Adam results in their expulsion from Eden, which is a symbol of the introduction of sin and anguish into the world. This expulsion is a consequence of the disobedience. According to Genesis 3:16-19, this expulsion represents not only a physical departure from paradise but also a spiritual estrangement from God. The challenges that Eve faced, such as the increased pain she experienced during childbirth and the complications that arose in her relationship with Adam, served to highlight the serious ramifications that their collective choice had on her life. Not only does the story show that disobedience results in personal anguish, but it also externalizes problems relating to societal relationships and roles. The repercussions that Eve experiences reverberate throughout theological debates regarding the nature of sin and the extent to which it is present in human experience. These discussions challenge readers to investigate the depth of human fallibility and divine justice (Wright, 2010).

The story of Eve in the Book of Genesis provides a thought-provoking analysis of companionship, free will, and the repercussions that come with making decisions. The creation of her symbolises the equality that she aspires to in her relationships, while the actions that she takes highlight the difficulties that are involved in making moral decisions when one is confronted with temptation. There are widespread effects of her disobedience throughout Judeo-Christian theology, which prompts deeper reflections on human nature, agency, and the regular challenges that come with living in accordance with divine will. Through our study of Eve's role, we can gain insights into the persistent debates that have arisen around sin, responsibility, and redemption. These debates illustrate the continuing significance of these challenges in the continuing investigation of moral philosophy.

# THE ROLE OF SARAH: FAITH AND DIVINE PROMISE

Sarah said, "God has brought me laughter, and everyone who hears about this will laugh with me." And she added, "Who would have said to Abraham that Sarah would nurse children? Yet I have borne him a son in his old age." (Genesis 21:6-7)

In the narrative of the Bible, Sarah is portrayed as an important person whose life is characterized by the topics of faith, doubt, and the promises made by God. Sarah's narrative is inextricably linked to the key occurrences that led to the establishment of the Abrahamic religions because she was married to Abraham and gave birth to Isaac. In the same way that Sarah underwent a metamorphosis in the scriptures, so too do the broader communal and divine changes that accompany the fundamental covenant that God made with Abraham regarding the name Sarai. The purpose of this chapter is to investigate Sarah's role as the first of the four Matriarchs, with a focus on the historical and religious context, the impact she had on religious tradition, and the various perspectives that bring to light her significance. In addition, it will examine the continuing impact of her narrative on current theological discussions and debates.

The narrative of Sarah exists within the broader context of the Ancient Near East, a period that was characterized by tribal migrations, the formation of religious identities, and the beginning stages of civilizations. To comprehend Sarah, it is necessary to investigate the world she inhabited, which was characterized by patriarchy and nomadism. There were significant cultural exchanges and migrations that occurred during this time, both of which influenced the formation of monotheism and helped to shape the biblical tale.

According to the Book of Genesis, Sarah is portrayed as an important person in the formation of a covenant with God, which is a divine promise that would have far-reaching consequences for her descendants. Beginning her adventure with Abraham in Ur of the Chaldees, she travels through Canaan and into Egypt. She does this as Sarai, which is the name of God. Even though women were depicted within a mostly male-dominated culture, her narrative emphasizes the significance of women in biblical society as advocates and participants in the works that God has planned (Fretheim, 1996).

In addition, Sarah's life is symbolic of the difficulties that women of her era encountered, such as infertility and concerns of self-worth. In her tale, she emphasizes experiences that are familiar to many women in the scripture, when problems of barrenness were found to be significant both socially and personally. According to Levenson (2015), this aspect of her narrative draws attention to the continuity that exists between the challenges that were raised in ancient scriptures and the present theological and cultural debates surrounding gender roles and families.

Faith is one of the most significant and well-defined themes that runs throughout Sarah's existence. The central focus of her narrative is the heavenly promise that she will become a mother when she is elderly. When Abraham and Sarah were given this promise, they were both shocked by its magnitude, so much so that it caused

Sarah to laugh at the possibility of it happening given her age. When faced with situations that appear to be insurmountable, her laughter, which is recognized by God and given the name Isaac, which means "he will laugh," is symbolic of the difficulty and complexity of faith.

Sarah's initial scepticism and her subsequent obedience to the promise of God highlight a dynamic and evolving faith experience. It is the human experience of trying to align hope with reality that is demonstrated by doubt, which acts as a catalyst for deeper faith and eventual belief. The narrative of her journey from doubt to confidence in divine providence not only enriches the narrative of the covenant but also provides a model for comprehending the faith journey.

In the traditions of Judaism, Christianity, and Islam, Sarah leaves behind a remarkable legacy. In her capacity as a matriarch, she is honoured for her devotion to God and for her contribution to the conception of Isaac, who is the one who continues the Abrahamic covenant. In the Jewish faith, Sarah is honoured throughout the reading of the Torah, particularly for her bravery and for the fact that her line was carried on through Isaac, her son. During services that are centred on the High Holy Days, her story is frequently retold, demonstrating the victory of faith over uncertainty (Blenkinsopp, 2008).

Sarah's life is a representation of faith in the context of Christianity. In the New Testament, specifically in Galatians 4, the Apostle Paul makes mention of her as a way of demonstrating how liberation and divine promise transcend human limitations. Her story is frequently interpreted as a forerunner to the teachings of the New Testament, which stress the importance of being patient and trusting in God's timing and plans (Witherington III, 2007).

In addition, Sarah is held in high esteem by the Islamic religion, which places an emphasis on her generosity and compassion. Even though it is not as prominently displayed as it is in the Bible, her tale makes a significant contribution to the understanding of the lineage from which Islamic traditions also originate, therefore reinforcing ideas of shared stories and ancestry. Across the theological and scholarly discourses, Sarah's narrative has been subjected to a wide variety of interpretations. Feminist theologians frequently discuss Sarah's agency, as well as her role in the biblical story as a woman who addresses and has an impact on the patriarchal structures of her time. Her narrative serves as a model for examining the roles and voices of women within sacred books, compelling contemporary readers to reassess traditional readings that may have the effect of obliterating the voices of women (Trible, 1978).

In addition, Sarah is a wonderful example of both resilience and transformational process. The multitude of her identities, ranging from Sarai to Sarah, serves as a symbol of the transformation and empowerment that is bestowed upon her because of her interaction with the divine. Faithfulness in the Face of Challenges: Her unshakable faith in the face of personal and cultural challenges inspires new interpretations of what it means to be faithful in the face of challenges.

There are also contemporary conversations surrounding infertility and the societal pressures that are associated with motherhood, and Sarah's story speaks to these issues. Her story provides insight into the psychological and spiritual hardships that are related with these problems by serving as a lens through which the tensions between the promises of God and human biology are examined.

In current religious, ethical, and cultural debates, Sarah's story continues to have a significant impact. The narrative of her life provides a useful framework for gaining a deeper understanding of the intricacies of faith, the problems that are inherent in human experience, and the interaction that exists between divine will and personal agency. Her role is not only the subject of theological discussion; it also has an impact on ethical questions pertaining to gender, family, and the social functions that have been established by historical pathways.

In the last few years, researchers have begun to use Sarah's narrative more frequently as a source of inspiration for broader discussions on interfaith dialogue, investigating the common roots and divergences that exist among the Abrahamic religions. As a matriarch, she fulfils the role of a leader who encourages others to recognize their common pasts while also respecting their different religious routes. The presence of this kind of dialogue is especially essential in the context of the world, as it promotes the development of mutual understanding and respect among communities of many different religions (Armstrong, 2007).

In the future, the legacy of Sarah may serve as a source of motivation for the continued re-evaluation of historical narratives with an emphasis on inclusive and diverse perspectives. Because we are becoming more aware of ancient civilizations and the intricate social and religious dynamics that they presented, Sarah can serve as a starting point for broader reflections on the ways in which the experiences of women are interwoven with the fabric of historical legacy and scripture.

However, even though Sarah's life is intertwined with ancient narratives, it continues to provide us with a deeper and more rich understanding of faith, identity, and the promises made by God. The perpetually challenge of maintaining faith in the face of life's ambiguities is highlighted by her transition from doubt to fulfilment. Her experiences and deeds serve as a model for subsequent generations, so influencing the faith traditions of millions of people as the first matriarch. Both the historical and theological studies that are being carried out regarding her life continue to be an essential component of comprehending human experience and divine contact as it is presented in the scripture. The account of Sarah, which is an essential component of the biblical story and possesses both a timeless and pertinent quality, continues to challenge, inspire, and provide hope to believers from all throughout the world and throughout all of time.

Not only does the change of name from Sarai to Sarah symbolize her new position, but it also reflects a fundamental transformation in her belief and identity. In Genesis 17:15-16, God says, "As for Sarai, your wife, you shall not call her name Sarai, but Sarah shall be the name that you shall give unto her." I will bestow my blessings upon her, and furthermore, I will grant you a son through her. The topics of promise and hope that she has throughout her life are strengthened by this divine pronouncement. In the beginning, Sarah demonstrates scepticism concerning the promise that God made to her regarding a child, which is found in Genesis 18:12. She laughs at the idea of conceiving a child when she is the age of being old. This laughter can be seen as a human response of doubt that resonates with many believers. It demonstrates the real difficulty that faith faces when confronted with situations that appear to be impossible (Walton, 2011).

As Sarah gives birth to Isaac when she is in her nineties, which is the realization of God's promise to Abraham, her position becomes increasingly more important. Her narrative is a perfect example of how God frequently calls people to endure difficulties before his promises are fulfilled. In the book of Genesis, chapter 21, verses 1 and 2, it says that "the Lord visited Sarah as he had said, and the

Lord did to Sarah as he had promised." The significance of patience and faith in relation to divine timing is highlighted by this, which not only reaffirms Sarah's position in God's redemptive tale but also does so. In addition, Sarah's laughter undergoes a transformation from doubt to joy, which is a manifestation of her acceptance of God's promise and her vital participation in God's covenant with Abraham. This transformation echoes the overarching biblical motif that faith invariably results.

The intricacy of Sarah's character reflects the broader emotional spectrum that comes with faith and doubt. Not only is her narrative relevant considering the historical context, but it also provides important spiritual lessons that are still applicable today. In her role as a model of faith, Sarah illustrates the point that uncertainty is an inherent component of the journey to faith. Sarah was able to receive power to conceive even when she was beyond the age of conception because she had faith in the one who had made the promise to her, according to Hebrews 11:11, which says that she received power to conceive. This passage conveys the core of her metamorphosis, depicting a woman who was subjected to ridicule and scepticism, yet in the end, she accepted the fulfilment of God's promise, according to Blenkinsopp (2015). As a result, Sarah's legacy serves as a source of motivation for many individuals in current faith contexts who are dealing with their own doubts.

# REBEKAH AS A PROPHETESS IN MIDRASH: INSIGHTS INTO DIVINE PURPOSE

And they blessed Rebekah and said to her, "Our sister, may you increase to thousands upon thousands; may your offspring possess the cities of their enemies." (Genesis 24:60)

Rebekah, a key figure in the Hebrew Bible's Book of Genesis, is notable for her influential role as the wife of Isaac and the mother of twin sons, Jacob, and Esau. The most important aspect of her legacy is the decisive actions that she took that changed the course of the biblical tale. This is especially true when it comes to gaining the familial blessing for Jacob instead of Esau, who was the one who was originally entitled to it. This chapter will investigate the historical context of her tale, as well as the influence that she had on the narrative and the theological repercussions, as well as discuss several perspectives on her character, and examine the continuing significance and interpretation of her deeds within the contexts of both academic and religious communities.

The first time Rebekah is mentioned in the biblical story is in Genesis 24, which is where her narrative begins with Abraham's servant attempting to find a wife for his son Isaac. Not only does Rebekah's responsiveness and willingness to become a member of Isaac's family reflect the social and cultural standards of the time, but it also demonstrates the early decisiveness and proactive personality that are characteristic of her character. This early representation lays the groundwork for her future deeds, which have a significant impact on the course that her family line will take.

Rebekah's deeds are presented against the background of the historical context of her own time. In the time that Rebekah lived, patriarchal systems were the norm, and women often had a restricted range of options available to them. Even considering these limitations, Rebekah comes across as a character who exercises a considerable amount of agency. The power dynamics that exist within family structures of the ancient Near East are brought to light by her actions that relate to her two sons. The intricacies of her narrative are reflective of the larger cultural concerns of inheritance, divine providence, and the complicated interaction between human free will and divine purposes, which are frequently reflected in scholarly interpretations (Meyers, 2013).

In addition to the role that she played in getting Isaac's blessing for Jacob, which was an act that was inspired by her understanding of divine prophecy that she had received many years earlier, Rebekah's narrative importance is further emphasized. The establishment of the Israelite lineage through Jacob makes this incident, which is described in Genesis 27, an important turning point in the theological storyline. Through her intervention, Rebekah demonstrates that she is a strategic thinker who is ready to take decisive actions to carry out what she believes to be the divine purpose. When it comes to biblical scholars and theologians, this aspect of her character evokes a variety of reactions. There are those who admire her for her inventiveness and steadfast devotion to what she believes to be the will of God, while others criticize her methods as being deceptive (Exum, 1990).

By strategically analysing Rebekah's choice, she is positioned within the spectrum of women in the Bible who challenge conventional roles to influence divine narratives. What is interesting is that her actions are supported by a personal assumption that is in line with the larger goals of the divine. Rebekah's narrative lends itself to a variety of interpretations that investigate the complex comprehension of moral ambiguity. These interpretations investigate the ways in which acts that are regarded as ethically troublesome might, in some cases, take place within biblical contexts to serve a higher purpose.

From a theological point of view, the narrative of Rebekah presents an interpretative challenge that has been reflected in a variety of religious teachings and debates surrounding the same topic. A variety of perspectives on her tale are provided by Jewish, Christian, and even Islamic traditions, which frequently use her story to explore topics such as destiny, divine involvement in human affairs, and the intricacies of love and loyalty within families. Considering the prophecy that she received while she was carrying him, which stated, "Two nations are in your womb," (Genesis 25:23), a lot of people believe that her favouritism toward Jacob is justified or explained. By virtue of this awareness, her actions are framed as being possibly essential to the development of a future that has been predetermined by the divine.

In addition, Rebekah's clear preference for Jacob over Esau brings up questions about maternal love, favouritism, and the unintentional effects that parental decisions can have on their children.

In addition to complicating straightforward moral assessments, her story invites readings that consider the larger narrative purpose that her actions may serve. Scholars have questioned whether her actions were driven by a genuine want to carry out the will of the divine or by more human factors, such as social standards or her own personal choice.

Rebekah's narrative continues to be a source of inspiration and a source of contemplation regarding women's agency within sacred texts, which is why it continues to be a relevant topic of discussion today. By acknowledging her as an active participant rather than a passive role in her own story, contemporary feminist viewpoints frequently challenge male-dominated interpretations of her by recognizing her as a figure of strength and ambition. As a result of these discussions, there is a greater incentive to re-read classical works of literature through perspectives that promote gender equality and that acknowledge the nuances of historical and religious stories (Trible, 1978).

Furthermore, it is possible to reflect on Rebekah's life and choices in contemporary times to assess the role of women in traversing family dynamics and leadership, both in religious and non-religious contexts. In the context of contemporary society, her assertiveness and initiative in determining the futures of her sons reflect broader themes of leadership and influence that continue to be relevant in discussions about gender roles.

Because interpretations of Rebekah's narrative continue to shift, they provide a rich opportunity to investigate the intersections of gender, religion, and power in ancient writings and the ways in which those texts are applied in contemporary contexts. Even though some people find her actions to be controversial, they serve as a testimony to the continuing complexity and multifaceted nature of biblical characters. These characters continue to captivate and inspire a variety of audiences.

Additional interdisciplinary approaches may be used in future research into the narrative of Rebekah. These approaches would make use of advancements in disciplines such as archaeology, anthropology, and literary theory to further expand understanding of her role and significance. The link between historical research and contemporary feminist theology can provide enriched viewpoints through academic exploration. This, in turn, fosters a deeper appreciation of the complexities surrounding biblical characters and the cultural contexts that influenced the narratives that shaped them.

In the narrative of Rebekah's marriage to Isaac, the Hebrew Bible's introduction of Rebekah in Genesis 24 highlights her strong character and assertiveness. In Genesis 24:19, she demonstrates her value and suitability as a partner for Isaac by taking the initiative to water the camels that belong to Abraham's servant. Not only does this first act demonstrate her compassion, but it also establishes the foundation for her subsequent significant choices that alter the narrative trajectory of her family. In addition, her ability to traverse familial connections and assert her power over her husband Isaac characterizes her as a figure of agency within a story that is mostly dominated by men.

Rebekah's most controversial action is her orchestration of the ruse that enables Jacob to receive the blessing that Isaac meant for Esau (Genesis 27). Rebekah alters the scenario by disguising Jacob in goat skins and presenting him as Esau to achieve what she believes to be a goal that is divinely assigned to her. The ethical implications of her strategies and the reasons for her actions are called into question by this act of deception. The readers' moral concerns often revolve around the actions she takes and the results that those actions produce. As a result of her belief in the prophecy that was given to her before to the birth of the twins (Genesis 25:23), she was able to see that her actions were essential to the completion of God's promise to Jacob.

Rebekah's swift reaction to the aftermath of the blessing theft is another demonstration of her loyalty to Jacob, which is evidenced by her swift response. To illustrate a mother's protective nature, she urged Jacob to run away to her brother Laban, who was staying in Haran (Genesis 27:43-45). On the other hand, this choice also results in a substantial estrangement between mother and son, which is a terrible outcome of her activities. The emotional intricacies of this separation serve to highlight the broader concept of familial disagreement that runs throughout the story of Genesis. In the end, Rebekah's loyalty proves to be both a source of strength and a source of demise for her, illustrating the complex interplay between the responsibilities of family and the quest of divine fulfilment.

Rebekah is a complex character in biblical literature, and her actions and motivations continue to provoke discussion and controversy. Readers are invited to think about the connections between divine prophecy, human agency, and family responsibility through the lens of her story, which is embedded within the patriarchal structure of the book of Genesis. Rebekah's influence and legacy continue to exist in both religious and academic dialogues, inspiring new generations to reinterpret ancient writings through a variety of contemporary perspectives. Not only does Rebekah continue to serve as a prominent example of women's active participation in the shaping of biblical history, but she also does so by recognizing the complexities of her tale and the depths of her character.

In the Book of Genesis, Rebekah's role is much more than that of a supporting character; it is much more than that. The story is shaped by her forceful personality and crucial choices, which illustrate aspects of faithfulness, deception, and divine care. Even though they are morally questionable, her actions in securing the blessing for Jacob serve to the realization of a larger divine purpose that highlights the intricacies of family relationships as depicted in biblical narratives. Even though Rebekah is no longer alive, she continues to be an important figure, and her legacy continues to inspire debates over the ramifications of her decisions within the larger context of the story told in Genesis.

# LEAH: THE MOTHER
# OF NATIONS

When the Lord saw that Leah was not loved, he enabled her
to conceive, but Rachel remained childless. (Genesis 29:31)

Leah's narrative, as told in the Bible, provides an intriguing
insight into family dynamics, divine intervention, and personal
transformation during the time of the patriarchs. Through this story,
one can see the complexities of family relationships. Leah, who was
married to Jacob first and was also the sister of Rachel, is famous
for being the mother of six of Jacob's sons: Reuben, Simeon, Levi,
Judah, Issachar, and Zebulun. Leah was also the first wife of Jacob.
This chapter delves into the historical context of Leah, the influence
she had on the biblical line, multiple interpretations of her narrative,
recent scholarly discussions regarding her role, and the significance
she will have in the future. Through an exploration of these facets,
the goal of this study is to illuminate Leah's continuing impact and
important position within the biblical story and beyond outside of
the biblical narrative.

Leah, who was Jacob's first wife and the elder sister of Rachel, is
a highly significant figure in the ancestry of the Israelite country.
As the mother of six of Jacob's sons—Reuben, Simeon, Levi,
Judah, Issachar, and Zebulun—of Jacob's sons themselves. Leah's
narrative is a microcosm of deep topics such as pregnancy, familial
competition, and the involvement of a higher power. Leah's

significance in the biblical story will be examined in this essay, with a particular focus on how her experiences reflect larger themes of legacy and divine favour, which in turn effect the establishment of Israel.

Leah's narrative takes place during a time in ancient history when family dynamics were patriarchal, and marriages sometimes included arrangements that ensured political or social alliances (Smith & Miller, 2012). Leah's narrative is predominantly recorded in the Book of Genesis, which reflects the social norms and values of the time regarding women, marriage, and domestic obligations. Leah's story is told in the Book of Genesis. In accordance with Genesis 29:23-27, Leah was provided to Jacob as a wife through the trickery of her father, Laban, who desired to marry off his older daughter, Rachel, before to marrying off his younger daughter, Rachel. Leah's life of rivalry with her sister and her fight for her husband's love are both influenced by this context, which sets the tone for her existence.

One of the reasons why Leah's role as a matriarch of the Israelites is so important is that she was the first four sons of Jacob, which laid the groundwork for the twelve tribes of Israel that would eventually emerge. Her sons Reuben, Simeon, Levi, and Judah are significant contributors to the history of the Israelite people. As an illustration, Levi is the ancestor of the Levitical priesthood, and the lineage of Judah is noteworthy because it has produced several important leaders, such as King David and, according to Christian belief, Jesus Christ.

Even though Leah struggled with her own issues, the narrative suggests that she became an important figure in the passing on of faith and heritage. In addition to showcasing deep-seated familial tensions, her marriage is also influenced by Jacob's favouritism towards Rachel and Leah's quest for love and acceptance, a struggle that has struck a chord with readers throughout history. It is Leah's resilience and devotion, both to her children and to God, that is the source of her enduring impact. This devotion is illustrated by the names she gives her boys and the prayers she offers for them.

Leah's most important contribution to the narrative of the Bible is in her role as a mother. Leah is the one who gives birth to the first six sons of Jacob, even though she is often eclipsed by her sister Rachel. In the ancient Near Eastern culture, the act of giving birth to children was rife with spiritual significance. It was seen as a symbol of motherhood as well as the perpetuation of one's own line (Ruth 4:11). Leah is seen as being favoured by God because of her ability to conceive, particularly because Rachel is having difficulty conceiving.

As an illustration, Leah's exclamation upon the delivery of her first child, Reuben, is suggestive of her desire for recognition. She exclaimed, "Because the Lord has seen my misery" (Genesis 29:32, New International Version). To grasp the emotional depth that Leah possesses, it is necessary to recognize the interplay between human suffering and divine favour.

In the context of the biblical worldview, the competition that exists between Leah and Rachel provides a multifaceted perspective through which to understand womanhood. Leah's perceived lack of beauty is frequently highlighted in contrast to Rachel's beauty, which serves to reinforce societal standards of value that are dependent on one's physical appearance. Not only is their rivalry for Jacob's love personal, but it also serves as a reflection of larger tensions that exist within familial arrangements (Genesis 30:1-2).

Leah frequently finds herself in a state of despair and desperation, leading her to measure her value by her capacity to give birth to male children. Leah, for instance, demonstrates her developing awareness of her worth beyond that of simple childbearing by stating, "This time I will praise the Lord" (Genesis 29:35, New International Version) after giving birth to Judah. The complexity of their relationship is revealed by this dynamic, as well as the consequences it will have for future generations.

There are a great number of interpretations that can be made of the biblical narrative of Leah, each of which offers a different lens through which to examine her personality. Leah's role as a devoted mother and wife is frequently highlighted in traditional readings, which place an emphasis on her dedication to carrying out her responsibilities within a marriage that was not always easy.

Leah's relationship with God is emphasized from a theological point of view, which suggests that her prayers and her eventual happiness are reflective of a profound spirituality that compensates for her lack of love for her married partner.

Leah's legacy, which includes her role as the mother of tribes, serves to highlight the significant contribution she made to the establishment of Israel. Her sons grow to become the patriarchs of major tribes, particularly Judah, from which King David and, according to the Christian faith, Jesus Christ are both descended.

Judah is one of the tribes that her sons oversee. Leah's important place within the Israelite story is confirmed by genealogies that appear throughout the Bible, which underscore the importance of Leah's ancestry (Matthew 1:2-3). There are elements of Leah's identity that are reflected in the characteristics of the tribes. For example, Leah's adoration of God may be linked to the name of her son, Judah, which implies that her spiritual legacy reflects the identity of the tribe itself. In this sense, Leah's life narrative is not just a private one, but it is also intimately connected to the identity and future of the state of Israel.

Leah is portrayed as a figure who is caught within the boundaries of patriarchal society, according to feminist scholars who offer an alternative perspective on Leah. The contrast between Leah's marginalized position and her significant contributions to Israelite culture is often used to illustrate how women's stories are influenced by the roles they are given and the societal expectations that are placed upon them (Brenner, 1997). This perspective enables a critical examination of how women's narratives are formed. In addition, Leah's narrative has been analysed from a psychological perspective, which involves examining her battle with favouritism and sibling rivalry. This perspective adds depth to the understanding of family dynamics and personal development (Sarna, 1995).

Scholars have engaged in critical reconsideration of Leah's tale over the past several years, investigating the ways in which biblical stories have been received and interpreted in contexts that are outside from the realm of conventional religious discourse. Leah is located within broader questions regarding the historicity of biblical characters, and contemporary research frequently investigates the historical accuracy of these accounts. The lived experiences of women during the time that is commonly linked with the Patriarchs are enhanced by the inclusion of archaeological findings that are relevant to this approach (Dever, 2002).

Leah's story is also becoming increasingly popular as a metaphor for social justice, which is another form of interest. Leah's marginalization and subsequent acknowledgment are framed by this interpretation as being symbolic of broader themes of justice and redemption through which Leah is marginalized. In contemporary debates concerning equity and moral integrity, her ascent to maternal prominence despite initial disregard serves as an illustration of bigger themes such as resilience and the eventual victory over injustice (Trible, 1978).

Leah's story in the Bible is a rich investigation of issues connected to fertility, rivalry, and the favour of God. Leah, who was Jacob's first wife, not only made a major contribution to the ancestors of the Israelite country but also personified the challenges that women encountered in situations where men oversaw everything. In the end, her journey demonstrates that her worth goes beyond the societal definitions of beauty and maternal achievement, therefore establishing her as a foundational character in the biblical storyline. Leah's legacy continues to reverberate, bringing attention to the intricacies of familial relationships as well as the broader history of Israel as a nation.

The account of Leah as it is told in the Bible is one that is both complex and resilient. Both the religious history and the literary studies emphasize her importance, as evidenced by her transformation from being rejected at first to becoming an important matriarch. Through the diverse lenses of historical context, theological interpretation, and contemporary scholarship, Leah emerges as a multifaceted character who continues to inspire and resonate with people across the world. Leah's story is a promise that it will continue to be relevant as scholars and theologians dig deeper into her tale. It will enhance our understanding of biblical history, cultural norms, and the enduring quest for love, acceptance, and a legacy that all humans embark on.

# THE COMPLEX LEGACY OF RACHEL: A STUDY OF BEAUTY, FAVOURITISM, AND STRUGGLE

So Jacob served seven years to get Rachel, but they seemed like only a few days to him because of his love for her. (Genesis 29:20)

In addition to being a story about love, family dynamics, and personal anguish, the narrative of Rachel as presented in the Bible is a vivid story. In the context of biblical history, Rachel is a significant figure because she is the daughter of Laban, the favourite wife of Jacob, and the mother of Joseph and Benjamin. Additionally, Rachel's tale is explored by examining the key elements that characterize her Biblical story, as well as investigating her influence on religious beliefs, literary influence, and her continuing relevance in contemporary times. In addition, Rachel's narrative illustrates a variety of perspectives, with an emphasis on the historical and theological interpretations and the ways in which her legacy continues to have an impact on current thought and practice.

In addition to her beauty and motherhood, Rachel holds a prominent role that extends beyond her role as Jacob's favourite wife. The broader topics of love, rivalry among women, and the intricacies of sacrifice are reflected in her relationships and experiences, which serve to encapsulate these themes. It is the argument of this chapter that the character of Rachel is a powerful, albeit tragic figure who reflects the gender relations and familial tensions of her time. Rachel is portrayed as a figure who embodies a blend of emotional depth and cultural dynamics within the patriarchal structure of Biblical Israel.

The Book of Genesis is where Rachel makes her appearance, and her life is intricately intertwined with that of the patriarch Jacob. In the narrative of the Bible, Jacob sees Rachel at the well and falls in love with her at first sight, selecting her as his preferred bride right then and there (Genesis 29:9-12). Jacob's journey to marriage with Rachel is beset with difficulties, even though he loves and is devoted to her. Jacob is tricked by her father, Laban, who replaces Leah, his elder daughter, for Rachel on the night of the wedding ceremony. As a result of this deception, Jacob is compelled to labour for an extra seven years to win Rachel's hand in marriage. This demonstrates the magnitude of his love as well as the significance that Rachel holds in his life (Genesis 29:18-30).

There is a vast difference between Rachel and her sibling Leah, which causes tension and rivalry, particularly regarding pregnancy and delivery. In Genesis 30:1-8, Rachel's lack of fertility is contrasted with Leah's fertility, which drives Rachel to offer her maidservant Bilhah to Jacob so that she may bear children on her behalf. This practice is referred to as surrogacy, which was common during that time. In later chapters, Rachel gives birth to two sons, Joseph, and Benjamin, both of whom play a significant role in the stories that are told in Genesis and in the subsequent historical accounts found in the Bible. Joseph is elevated to a prominent position, depicted as a leader in Egypt and a dream interpreter (Genesis 37, 39-50).

Jacob's affections are hugely impacted by the central component of Rachel's personality, which is her beauty. The New International

Version of the Bible (NIV) states that she was "beautiful in form and appearance" (Genesis 29:17), which implies that Jacob's love for her over his love for her sister Leah was influenced by her physical qualities. The favouritism shown to one sister over the other creates a rivalry between them, resulting in a nasty relationship that reverberates throughout their entire lives. Leah's emotions of inadequacy serve as a commentary on the social pressures that women face to attain both love and approval from their husbands. These pressures are reflected in Leah's feelings of inadequacy. Alter (2011) argues that the rich emotional terrain that is created by this rivalry serves to not only highlight the beauty of Rachel, but also to illustrate the traumatic effects that the rivalry between the two sisters has on their understanding of their challenges.

Rachel's identity as a mother is a significant component of her story, and it is particularly emphasized by her desperate want to become a mother of children. Rachel's supplication to Jacob, which translated to "Give me children, or I shall die!" (Genesis 30:1, ESV), highlights the social pressure that is put on women to conceive children. Rachel was confronted with the issue of infertility. To fulfil her desire of becoming a mother, she is willing to traverse social conventions, as evidenced by her offering her maid, Bilhah, to Jacob as a gift. Not only does the birth of Joseph and Benjamin represent the realization of Rachel's personal ambitions, but it also symbolizes her eventual connection to the larger narrative of the history of the nation of Israel. Joseph, who is regarded as a favoured child, plays a significant role in the narrative of the Israelites. He is a symbol of Rachel's victorious yet heart-breaking legacy, which is marked by her death as she gives birth to Benjamin (Brueggemann, 2008).

The conclusion of Rachel's narrative is a tragedy, as she passes away during the labour and delivery of her second son, who is named Benjamin. The theme of love and loss is strengthened by her passing, which intertwines joy and sorrow and emphasizes the delicate nature of human life, as seen in Genesis 35:16-20. Her passing away signifies the conclusion of her immediate impact; yet it also marks the beginning of a new chapter in her legacy through her children. While she is passing away, she gives her son the name Ben-Oni, which literally translates to "son of my sorrow." This name reflects the profound emotional upheaval that she is experiencing as well as the agony that she is going through during labour. Despite this, Jacob gives him the name Benjamin, viewing the situation through a perspective of survival and hope, as stated in Genesis 35:18 of the New International Version. The duality of Rachel's legacy is symbolized by this transformation: while her life was characterized by love and beauty, it also came to an end in heartache. The death of Rachel has a profound influence on the Israelite identity and its familial structures, as it serves to reinforce the themes of sacrifice and the great stakes of motherhood within a patriarchal society (Frymer-Kensky, 2002).

The story of Rachel is not only a family drama; rather, it provides a platform for the investigation of larger theological and cultural issues. In terms of history, Rachel's narrative is indicative of the social standards and behaviours that were prevalent during her time. The cultural context of ancient Near Eastern societies encompassed intricate family structures and marital arrangements, as shown in the narrative of Jacob, Leah, and Rachel, as well as in the marriages of Jacob, Leah, and Rachel. The story of surrogacy that is portrayed in Rachel's narrative provides insights into the historical societal values that were held (Meyers, 2013). This example illustrates the lengths that people would go to ensure that their lineage and legacy were secured.

Rachel is not only a representation of beauty and love in a theological sense, but her narrative also addresses issues such as jealousy, the privileged position she possessed, and the involvement of God. Her life is a testament to the fact that deeply intimate desires, such as Rachel's desire for children and Jacob's devotion for her, are inextricably interwoven with divine stories of promise and fulfilment. Throughout the history of Jewish literature, Rachel's role has been emphasized, with particular emphasis placed on her compassion and her intercession for her children. This is evident even after her passing, as seen in the Jewish traditions that portray Rachel mourning for the children of Israel who have been exiled (Jeremiah 31:15).

Through the ages, Rachel's influence has extended beyond the scope of the Biblical narrative, infiltrating religious thought, literature, and cultural manifestations in various forms. Many literary and artistic works have been influenced by her character, which has contributed to the establishment of her enduring legacy. In both Christianity and Judaism, Rachel is frequently regarded as the model of motherhood and is linked to feelings of love and grief that are associated with motherhood. It is reported that her grave is in Bethlehem, and it continues to be a popular pilgrimage destination, which demonstrates the enduring spiritual impact that she has had.

To summarize, the narrative of Rachel in the Bible is a compelling investigation into the various aspects of love, competition, motherhood, and sacrifice. Rachel is a multifaceted character who embodies the challenges and heartaches that women experience in a patriarchal society. This is illustrated by her relationships with Jacob and Leah, as well as her ultimate sacrifice as a mother. Her narrative not only serves to deepen our understanding of specific characters in the biblical text, but it also embodies the larger cultural dynamics that were in play during her time. As a result, she is an essential figure in the formation of Israel's national identity.

Scholars and theologians continue to conduct research on the narrative of Rachel in search of insights that pertain to both the problems that were faced in antiquity and those that are faced today. Modern debates regarding family dynamics and the position of women in religious texts are resonant with issues such as infertility, identity development, favouritism, and family conflicts. The intricacy of her encounters and relationships creates a rich ground for feminist and historical discourse, which strives to uncover the subtleties of her story within the patriarchal framework of the Bible (Trible, 1984).

A multi-faceted understanding of the significance of Rachel may be gained through the exploration of her narrative from a variety of different perspectives. The agency and voice of Rachel have been investigated by feminist scholars within the context of her patriarchal society, which has led to wider discussions about gender roles in religious texts. Not only do these contemporary viewpoints serve to reframe established interpretations, but they also offer new views that are in line with the current discussions that are taking place around gender and equality.

The narrative of Rachel remains timely as society progresses, which invites both its reinterpretation and its renewed interest. When it comes to the treatment of her story in the contexts of education and religion, there is an ongoing difficulty to reflect contemporary values while also remaining true to the scriptural texts. The historical figures of the Bible, such as Rachel, are often used as a source of inspiration by academic research and theological workshops when it comes to addressing concerns such as the ethical dilemmas faced by women, the rights of women, and the psychological insights into human behaviour.

In addition, the development of digital humanities and increased access to Biblical texts and commentaries online could further enhance exploration into her life and the effects that it has had. It is possible that technological advancements will provide even more opportunities for collaboration between academics and members of the public, inviting a shared investigation into the textual complexities that are related to Rachel's life.

Rachel's narrative is deeply infused with complexities that revolve around love, conflict, and the search for fulfilment, encompassing both the human and divine aspects of existence. The impact that she has had continues to reverberate throughout time, and it continues to capture the imagination of religious believers, academics, and cultural interpreters all around the world. By looking at Rachel's life from a historical, theological, and contemporary point of view, we acknowledge her as an important figure whose story continues to provoke thought about ancient social standards and current human challenges.

The narrative of Rachel in the Bible is a strong investigation into the many different aspects of love, rivalry, motherhood, and sacrifice. Rachel is a multifaceted character who embodies the hardships and tragedies that women face in a patriarchal society. Through her relationships with Jacob and Leah, as well as her ultimate act of sacrifice as a mother, Rachel illustrates the difficulties and tragedies that women endure. By portraying the broader cultural forces that were in play during her time, her story makes her a significant figure in the formation of Israel's national identity. It not only adds to the understanding of individual characters in the biblical text but also enriches the context of those characters.

# THE ROLE OF MIRIAM: A LEADER IN EXODUS 15:20-21

Then Miriam the prophet, Aaron's sister, took a
timbrel in her hand, and all the women followed her,
with timbrels and dancing. (Exodus 15:20)

Miriam, who is a major character in the stories of the Bible, is most
often seen in the context of the Exodus story, where she is depicted
as the older sister of Moses and Aaron and as the prophetess.
She is depicted in the Bible as a symbol of protection and direct
leadership, where she manifests as a protector of her brother Moses
and a leader among the Israelites, particularly during their difficult
escape from Egyptian bondage. Her presence in the Bible is filled
with symbolism. This chapter investigates the many roles and
contributions that Miriam had, including her influence within the
historical and cultural context of the Exodus, her leadership roles,
and her enduring impact on religious and feminist interpretations.

Although the precise dates vary amongst historians, the narrative of
Miriam takes place during a time that is often believed to be about
the 13th century BCE. Her story is interwoven with one of the most
significant and dramatic occurrences in the history of the Jewish
people: the Exodus from Egypt. Miriam's prominent position is more
impressive given the patriarchal context of the ancient societies
of the Near East. Her actions take place at a time that is crucial for

the Israelites, and her leadership and visions serve as a compass for them in terms of morals and spirituality.

In the Biblical passage of Exodus 2:1-10, Miriam is introduced for the first time, albeit without being called initially. She is the sister who plays a role in rescuing the baby Moses. It is Miriam who is responsible for watching over Moses when their mother, Jochebed, puts him in a basket to escape the Pharaoh's order to drown all Hebrew male infants. The fact that she proposed her mother to be Moses' nurse is what lays the groundwork for his survival and his subsequent rise as a leader (Exodus 2:4-9). In the words of Zornberg (2011), Miriam's watchful presence and strategic thinking are two qualities that exemplify her bravery and resourcefulness.

After Moses was called to be a leader and after they fled Egypt, Miriam made another appearance in one of the key events that took place after the crossing of the Red Sea. In Exodus 15:20-21, she encourages the women of Israel to sing a song of celebration, which is generally known as the "Song of the Sea." This event establishes her as a spiritual leader and the first female prophetess according to the Hebrew Bible. Exodus 15:20 states that "Then Miriam the prophetess, the sister of Aaron, took a tambourine in her hand, and all the women followed her, with tambourines and dancing." This is what the scripture says. The celebration expressed in this song is more than just an expression of joy; it is also an expression of gratitude and recognition of the help provided by God through a communal act. Some academics, including Meyers et al. (2005), believe that the leadership and inspiration that she provides currently reflects her ability to unite the community through the principles of religion and celebration (Meyers et al. 2005).

An excellent example of Miriam's leadership and influencing

abilities within the Israelite community is provided by her leading the Israelite women in song following their escape from Egypt, as described in Exodus 15:20-21. Not only does Miriam serve as a sister to Moses, but her actions are also reflective of her position as a vital actor in the spiritual and cultural life of her community. Miriam's act embodies strong leadership qualities that cultivate a sense of identity and resilience within the community, making her a key character in the Exodus story and beyond. The song sung by Miriam not only praises the intervention of the divine but also calls for participation and solidarity among the women. In the end, it serves to reinforce the significance of collective memory and worship in shaping the experiences of the Israelites.

During the time when she is miraculously escaping from Pharaoh's grip, Miriam demonstrates her leadership by singing with her fellow Israelites. This is an example of how she navigates the feelings of her fellow Israelites through her singing. It is written in Exodus 15:20-21 that she took a timbrel in her hand and encouraged the ladies to join her in singing praises together. It is possible to interpret this action as a catalytic moment that turns a group that is afraid into a collective that celebrates their emancipation together. According to Alter (2008), the communal aspect of her leadership is clear, as each woman sings the same song as she does. This demonstrates the significance of collective worship in expressing thanks to God. Miriam's position is essential, as it exemplifies how leadership may be manifested in creative ways and artistic expression. It highlights the strength of music as an instrument for bringing people together and fostering community solidarity.

Miriam's actions reveal a deeper theological significance, portraying her as a prophetic figure who is aware of the ramifications that come with the deliverance of Israel from sin. Miriam not only gives recognition to the mighty deeds of God by leading the women in song, but she also takes an active role in the empowering of faith and hope among her people through her actions. Although men are often cast in most leadership roles according to the biblical narrative, Miriam is an exception to the rule. She is a female who takes the initiative to involve women in a communal expression of faith. This is a clear challenge to traditional gender roles. The purpose of this prophetic declaration made through music is to strengthen the identity of the Israelite community and to empower the voices of women within religious contexts. It serves as an example of how women can play important positions in spiritual and social leadership.

From a theological standpoint, the depiction of Miriam alongside her siblings Moses and Aaron situates her within a triadic leadership paradigm that is essential to the survival and spiritual journey of the Israelite people. In challenging narratives that are purely patriarchal, it proposes that women be included in important religious positions. She conjures up collective memory through her song and dance, so shaping Israel's sense of identity and their devotion to the divine will (Frymer-Kensky, 1992).

There are complexities that are inherent to Miriam's contributions. At the very least, her participation in the Numbers 12 episode of Numbers 12 underscores tensions even at the most senior levels of leadership. Miriam and Aaron raise their voices against Moses regarding his wife from Cush, calling into question the singular prophetic experience that Moses had. Considering this, Miriam is afflicted with leprosy, which is interpreted by different academics in different ways. Some believe it is the result of divine punishment for opposing male authority, while others believe it is a political strategy to combat dissent within the leadership (Plaut & Stein 2015). However, the fact that she was healed immediately following Moses' supplication to God serves to reaffirm her significance. Her absence from the community for a week resulted in a halt in the Israelites' journey, which demonstrates the important role she plays within the community (Numbers 12:13-15).

There is a significant amount of continued relevance that Miriam's narrative has in present discussions around leadership and gender roles. Her story has been a source of motivation for feminist theologians and academics who are seeking for representation and equality within religious traditions through its illustrative model. Gafney (2017) argues that Miriam's multiplicitous roles as a leader, teacher, and prophetess provide a challenge to traditional male interpretations of the Bible. Gafney goes on to say that this perspective expands our understanding of women's contributions in religious writings (Gafney, 2017).

Miriam's leadership is a model for future generations, as it extends beyond her immediate surroundings and context. Her act of leading the ladies in singing is a demonstration of empowerment and resilience, since it demonstrates how individuals can rise to inspire communities during times of hardship. The fact that her song is commemorated in a holy text is a testament to the enduring influence that she has had on others. Miriam's song, according to biblical scholars, is the foundation of Israel's national identity and collective memory (Kugel, 2001). By using the arts to bridge the gap between past experiences and present worship practices, this example demonstrates the significance of remembering one's own faith and ancestry through the creative expression of art, therefore establishing her position as an integral part of Israel's cultural heritage.

The impact that Miriam had may be observed in the Jewish tradition as well as other traditions throughout history. The "Miriam's Cup," which was added to certain Passover ceremonies, is a symbol of the everlasting significance of Miriam, as well as a recognition of the contributions that women have made to the history and spirituality of the Jewish faith. In a similar vein, her story has struck a chord within the Christian tradition, where her leadership qualities are brought out in conversations about faith and community development.

The symbols and motifs that are related with Miriam, the tambourine, the water, the song, and other aspects of life-giving, celebration, and prophetic insight are frequently the subject of theological discourse. This discourse investigates the ways in which these symbols and motifs extend her influence beyond historical accounts. These symbols go beyond basic meanings, implying metaphoric avenues for the formation and maintenance of communities. According to Levenson (1995), these components are seen as focal points that help to the communal mindset of collective identity and liberation (Levenson, 1995).

Looking ahead, the narrative of Miriam has the potential to significantly impact the development of religious practices and ecumenical conversations going forward. Her story has the potential to inspire an expanded incorporation of women into leadership positions within religious organizations, and it also serves as a catalyst for the ongoing investigation of gender roles within religious texts. The lessons that can be learned from Miriam's leadership and spirituality can also be applied to interfaith dialogue, where they can serve as a foundation for comprehending common histories and principles.

The narrative of Miriam continues to generate discussion within academic circles regarding the role of female figures in ancient texts, which in turn influences the way Bible studies and theological discourses are taught. Her narrative has the potential to stimulate new interpretive strategies that re-evaluate women's agency within the scriptures, in addition to expanding upon traditional understandings of prophethood and communal leadership.

Miriam is a compelling character in the biblical story, and she is a tribute to the significant influence that women have had throughout history, even in male-dominated environments. In addition to promoting justice and inclusivity, her leadership, vision, and moral fortitude provide a profound example of faith-based leadership. Miriam's legacy as a leader of faith and cultural significance continues to endure even as scholarly interest in her narrative continues to develop. This legacy encourages a re-evaluation of gender roles and spiritual leadership in both historical and contemporary contexts. Using song and collective expression, Miriam exemplified a multidimensional approach to leading her people, as seen in Exodus 15:20-21. This approach is reflected in her leadership style.

By her actions, she cultivates a feeling of togetherness and belonging, which serves to strengthen both the spiritual and cultural identities of the Israelite women. In addition, Miriam's position has the potential to challenge established gender norms and set a standard for the involvement of women in leadership positions within sacred contexts. A vibrant model for leadership that stresses innovation, faith, and community solidarity is presented by Miriam's initiative, which is revealed through the analysis of her legacy that extends beyond the historical narrative that she has left behind.

# THE FAITH OF RAHAB: A STUDY OF REDEMPTION AND LEGACY

By faith the prostitute Rahab, because she welcomed the spies, was not killed with those who were disobedient. (Hebrews 11:31)

As described in the Book of Joshua, the narrative of Rahab holds a significant position within the context of biblical history and theology. Rahab, who was born a prostitute in Jericho, made the decision to assist the spies from Israel during their mission, which ultimately resulted in the deliverance of her family during the attack on the city. The narrative of Rahab is the focus of this chapter, which delves into historical contexts, investigates different points of view, and considers the wider consequences for faith and genealogy. Faith, redemption, and social inversion are three major topics that are woven throughout the narrative of Rahab in the Book of Joshua.

By sheltering Israelite spies, Rahab the prostitute in Jericho played a key role in the Israelite invasion, which challenged prevailing social standards relating to faith and ethics. Her actions brought attention to her important position in the conquest. In addition to solidifying her significance, the fact that she is included in the lineage of Jesus suggests that faith goes beyond social classifications and origins. The account of Rahab, as told in the Book of Joshua, is a powerful story of faith, redemption, and the subversion of social standards. It ultimately portrays Rahab as a prominent person in biblical history as well as in the genealogy of Jesus Christ.

The Book of Joshua is the primary source of information regarding Rahab's tale. Because Jericho was a stronghold that stood in the way of Israel's assertion to the promised land, Joshua was intent on developing a clever strategy to overcome this hurdle (Joshua 2:1-21). Rahab, who resided on the city wall, was instrumental in the execution of this plan by concealing the Israelite spies who were dispatched to reconnoitre the city. Her bravery and faith were crucial. Because of the faith and redemption that she exemplifies through her actions, she is included in the genealogy of Jesus Christ.

Our understanding of Rahab's significance is improved when we have a better understanding of the historical context in which she lived. In the days of Rahab, Jericho was not only one of the oldest cities in the world but also a city of significant military and commercial importance. There were considerable defences at the city because it was in the plain of the Jordan Valley. As a result, it naturally became a strategic target for Israel (Bright, 2000).

During the period known as the Late Bronze Age, which is believed to be the time in which Rahab's tale was set, Canaan was a dispersed area that was controlled by a variety of city-states. The king of Jericho, as well as the citizens of Jericho, was disturbed by the presence of the Israelites. According to Mazar and his colleagues (1990), the presence of this impending danger was what led to Rahab's crucial choice.

In addition, the perceptions of prostitutes that existed during this period serve to further emphasize the important role that Rahab played. Rahab's ability to go from the periphery of society to a central role in the Israelite story is a demonstration of the potential for profound transformation and divine providence, even though she was a member of a marginalized group (Brenner, 2014).

The journey that Rahab took from exclusion to salvation is a testament to the power of faith. Although she was a prostitute and a Gentile, her proclamation to the spies that "the Lord your God is God in heaven above and on the earth below" (Joshua 2:11) is a testament to the deep faith that she possessed. Purity, worthiness, and divine selection are challenged by the central themes of grace and redemption that are emphasized in the biblical story.

Rahab's faith not only enabled her to alter the course of her own life, but it also allowed her to contribute to the larger redemptive story that runs throughout the biblical record. According to the Gospel of Matthew (Matthew 1:5), her ancestry includes Jesus, which serves as a demonstration of the universality of God's covenantal promises. In this instance, her narrative lends support to the idea that divine love and compassion go beyond human social creations and shortcomings.

In Joshua 2:11, Rahab proclaims her trust in the God of Israel, which is a clear example of her faith. This verse describes how she conceals the spies from Israelite and proclaims her belief. In addition to exhibiting a radical transformation in loyalty from her own people to the God of Israel, Rahab not only refuses the expectations of her society by choosing to protect these men, but she also demonstrates this shift. When she petitions the spies for a sign of mercy for her family, demonstrating her readiness to put her own life in jeopardy in the hopes of being saved, this act of faith is brought out even more. The purpose of this narrative is to encourage readers to rethink the definition of faith not only as a static conviction but rather as an active choice that has the potential to bring about life-altering results.

In the genealogy of Jesus that is presented in the Gospel of Matthew, Rahab is listed as one of his forebears, which serves to underscore her significance. Tamar, Rahab, Ruth, and Bathsheba are the four women that Matthew specifically singles out in this lineage. Not only does Rahab's inclusion serve as a testament to her faithfulness, but it also serves to reinforce the message that God has the power to redeem and employ all people, regardless of the history that they have (Carson, 1999).

The incorporation of such values is consistent with broader theological discussions around inclusiveness and salvation. The fact that there are Gentile women in the lineage of Jesus challenges interpretations of God's promises that are exclusive and points to the universal scope of the gospel message. Rahab's devotion serves as a model for believers, demonstrating the power of faith, perseverance, and the capacity for transformation that can be achieved through the intervention of God.

The numerous interpretations of Rahab's story that have been offered by theologians and scholars have had an impact on broader discussions concerning biblical figures and the functions they play in the framework of divine salvation history. According to Trible (2022), feminist theologians frequently consider her narrative to be an empowering tribute to women's agency in the context of a patriarchal social system. In the act of deciding to assist the Israelite spies, Rahab demonstrates independence and bravery, challenging the gender norms and social expectations that are imposed upon her.

A compelling example of redemption is found in the narrative of

Rahab. Although she was a prostitute, the acts that she took were in accordance with the divine purpose, which resulted in the salvation of not only herself but also her family, as stated in Joshua 6:25. The idea of redemption is an important one since it implies that one's history does not have to define their upcoming experiences. Rahab is an example of the potential for transformation that faith may provide. She is saved and incorporated into the community of Israelites after being saved. The fact that she is subsequently included in the lineage of Christ (Matthew 1:5) serves to reinforce this argument, which is that God can use anyone, no matter what they have done in the past.

The narrative of Rahab serves to challenge and undermine the societal standards that govern identity and value. Rahab is a model of strength and agency in a patriarchal culture that frequently discriminated against women, especially those who worked in her field. Her decision to act on behalf of the spies from Israel is an example of a defiance of gender norms and social expectations that is both proactive and presenting a woman who plays a vital role in the fate of a nation (Gafney, 2017). Not only does this inversion of traditional roles exemplify her bravery, but it also acts as a wider commentary on the comprehensiveness of God's purpose, which allows for people from all walks of life to take part in divine stories with God.

In addition, Christian interpretations highlight Rahab as a forerunner to the universality that is proclaimed in the New Testament. According to Witherington (2001), her tale is a good illustration of the idea that faith, regardless of one's cultural background, can align individuals with God's redemptive plan. This idea has been echoed throughout the theological landscape and in interfaith dialogues.

Current scholarly investigation continues to dissect the legacy of

Rahab, examining the ways in which early Christian and Jewish traditions differently perceive her narrative through various lenses. Archaeological evidence is being evaluated by several current scholars to reconcile the Jericho story with historical data, which adds additional layers of complexity to the interpretation of her story (Kenyon, 1987).

Throughout the course of history, well-known theologians have offered a variety of perspectives on the relevance of Rahab. Saint Augustine and Martin Luther, for example, cited the faith of Rahab as an example of the doctrine of justification by faith, which is a fundamental teaching of Christian theology (Lane, 2007). Both interpretations lend support to the effectiveness of her narrative in reinforcing doctrinal and liturgical discourse.

In the context of Jewish academic traditions, the Talmud praises Rahab for her high level of intelligence and insight. Many rabbinic traditions emphasize her foresight, citing her knowledge and intelligence even though she was of a low social standing. In these stories, Rahab is portrayed as someone who is not passive, but rather as someone who is actively influencing Israel's victory against Jericho.

Faith, identity, and redemption are all topics that are opened for discussion through the analysis of Rahab's narrative. Her tale serves as a catalyst for ongoing theological reflection on the ways in which marginalized groups participate within religious stories, with the goal of expanding inclusion and dialogue. In addition, the intersection of text and history may provide additional insights, particularly as scriptural studies incorporate discoveries from archaeological research.

Ongoing theological and archaeological efforts have the potential to further expand our understanding of the time of Rahab as well as the subtleties that are found within the biblical writings. Interfaith conversations take their cue from the journey that Rahab took, and they seek to foster a sense of mutual respect and understanding among differing theological faiths and interpretations.

Within the biblical texts, the story of Rahab is still a compelling tale that highlights important topics such as faith, redemption, and the inclusiveness of God. The transition of her from an outsider to a key person in the history of the Bible is a testament to the transformative power of faith and God's plan for bringing about change and restoration. Both scholars and practitioners of religion find a demonstration of the universality and accessibility of divine love and mercy in the process of deriving lessons from her life.

# THE LEADERSHIP OF DEBORAH IN THE HEBREW BIBLE: FEMALE EMPOWERMENT AND DIVINE INSIGHT

"Now Deborah, a prophet, the wife of Lappidoth, was leading Israel at that time. She held court under the Palm of Deborah between Ramah and Bethel in the hill country of Ephraim, and the Israelites went up to her to have their disputes decided." (Deborah 4:4-5)

In the Hebrew Bible, Deborah is portrayed as a model of leadership, wisdom, and bravery. She is the only female judge and prophet mentioned in the Book of Judges, and she is credited with playing a significant role in the Israelite's struggle against the Canaanite forces of oppression. The purpose of this chapter is to investigate the historical context of Deborah's tale, the influence that she had on her people and the overarching story of the Bible, as well as her legacy as an influential woman in religious and historical discussions.

We will investigate the complexities of her leadership through a detailed analysis of her story, evaluate a variety of academic viewpoints, and consider her significance in relation to current debates regarding leadership and gender through our research. An outstanding story of feminine empowerment and influence within a patriarchal framework is provided by her leadership during a period of repression and oppression. The narrative of Deborah illustrates how her leadership motivated the Israelites to revolt against their oppressors, the Canaanites, and finally achieve victory against them. This essay will investigate the many roles that Deborah played, analyse the contributions that she made to the society of the Israelites, and assess the ways in which her legacy continues to be relevant in present debates regarding female leadership.

The narrative of Deborah takes place in the Book of Judges, which is a scripture that belongs to the Deuteronomistic history. This history was written during the Late Bronze Age, between 1200 and 1020 BCE. During Canaanite rule, this was a period that was marked by socio-political turmoil, tribal hostilities, and the struggle of the Israelites to establish themselves in the Promised Land. The Israelites tended to conflict with their neighbours, and their security was frequently jeopardized by forces from outside their own country.

The story begins with Deborah appearing at a time when Israel is experiencing severe misery at the hands of Jabin, the king of Canaan, and his military commander, Sisera. This is the time when Israel is coming under the harsh oppression of Jabin. Deborah's leadership is a dual role that highlights her spiritual prowess as well as her administrative capabilities. She is both a prophetess and a judge (Younger, 2021). The story of Deborah does not adhere to the customary pattern of sin and redemption that is seen in the stories of the other judges in the Book of Judges. Instead, it places an emphasis on moral and spiritual leadership.

When it comes to leadership styles, Deborah challenges the traditional gender norms of her day. According to Judges 4:5, she commands her court under the Deborah Palm in the mountainous region of Ephraim, where the Israelites go to her to have their disagreements resolved. Her position reflects her recognition as a leader with divine insight and authority, which stands in contrast to the patriarchal social system that was common in the ancient Near East.

Against the Canaanites, Deborah engages in military activity that is both strategic and critically important to their cause. Following a revelation that she received from God, she summons Barak and requests that he assemble an army of ten thousand soldiers to go into battle against Sisera's forces. In Judges 4:8, Barak makes it clear that he wants Deborah to accompany him into battle. This is a significant demonstration of her leadership, as her presence guarantees that the troops will have divine favour and morale.

There are major implications that Deborah's story has for the Israelites' comprehension of leadership and divine involvement with them. Not only does her successful military strategy result in a key victory, but it also acts as a reaffirmation of the authority bestowed upon her by prophecy. The triumph over Sisera, which was made possible by a complex plan that took advantage of a nearby thunderstorm, is a symbolic representation of the victory that faith and divine intervention have over the power of professional military forces.

In addition, the song that Deborah sings in Judges 5 provides an epic account of the battle and serves to reinforce her important role in the liberation of the Israelites. Her hymn, which is one of the earliest extant Hebrew poems, is a literary masterpiece that not only reflects her triumph but also embodies the cultural and philosophical spirit of the age. As a result of her song, Deborah serves as a channel for the collective memory and cultural identity of the Israelite people.

Most significantly, Barak and Jael are among the others with whom Deborah works together, which is a significant aspect of her leadership. Even though Deborah was given divine wisdom and power, she did not accomplish her goals in solitude. In the case of Barak, he is a model of the conjunction of faith and action, whereas Jael's decisive act in killing Sisera with a tent peg illustrates the unanticipated means of salvation, as stated in Judges 4:21.

The complexity of leadership is demonstrated through these interactions, which highlight the significance of collective action as well as the significance of individual initiative. Deborah's partnership with Barak and her tribute to Jael in her triumph song (Judges 5:24-27) are two examples of an inclusive leadership style that goes beyond gender and class divisions.

There are multiple interpretations of Deborah's legacy in the fields of religion, feminism, and cultural studies. Her legacy is enduring and multifaceted. Her narrative not only challenges conventional gender roles, but it also continues to raise questions about female agency and authority in religious texts (Ackerman, 1998) because she is a female leader in a male-dominated narrative.

Deborah's story has been restudied in recent times as an example of leadership that is not limited by gender that is not confined by gender. Her narrative is found in modern discussions about gender equality, which urge for a re-evaluation of ancient books to highlight the roles that women played in historical and religious contexts.

The fact that Deborah is the only female judge who is mentioned in the Hebrew Bible is a demonstration of her unique position in a society that was largely dominated by men. In her capacity as a judge, she possessed a great deal of power, as she was responsible for resolving conflicts and offering counsel to the Israelites. According to Judges 4:5, she would sit beneath a palm tree that was called the Palm of Deborah, and people would come to her for judgment. Not only does her existing public presence serve as a sign of her respected position, but it also serves as a sign of her role as a key figure in the community, where she exerts both spiritual and secular authority. Not only does Deborah's exceptional ability to govern effectively dispel the idea that women did not have power in ancient cultures, but it also presents a contrast to broader historical narratives that have been presented.

The portrayal of Deborah as a prophetess emphasizes her important involvement in inspiring the Israelites against the Canaanites by depicting her as receiving divine revelation. When she urges Barak to gather an army, she is demonstrating her prophetic authority to lead others (Judges 4:6). She not only provides him with tactical instructions, but she also assures him that their mission will have the support of God. As an illustration, Deborah's assertion that "the Lord will go ahead of you" is a sign of her trust in the power of divine intervention, which is a crucial component in maintaining morale among her constituents. Her capacity to transcend traditional gender roles is highlighted by the strategic brilliance with which she orchestrates their military response against Sisera, the commander of the Canaanites. This position positions her as both a spiritual leader and a tactical planner for the invasion.

In current debates surrounding female leadership and empowerment, Deborah's story carries a major amount of weight. Because it challenges existing historical narratives that ignore women's contributions in positions of leadership, her story is frequently cited in feminist theological discourse. In addition,

Deborah's victory song, which was inspired by her victory over Sisera (Judges 5), portrays her as a champion of communal identity and celebration, which further cements her legacy. Not only does the song narrate the battle, but it also acts as a reflection of the power dynamics that existed in ancient Israel, including the repercussions of a woman's leadership when she was in a transformational position. For this reason, Deborah is not only a figure who had an impact on her immediate surroundings, but she also serves as a source of inspiration for future generations as they strive for equality and justice.

In addition, Deborah's leadership has been evaluated considering the findings of current organizational research. According to Northouse (2021), her narrative provides useful insights into transformational leadership, which is characterized by an emphasis on vision, inspiration, and moral integrity rather than on simply specific positional power. Deborah's ability to bring together a variety of tribal groups under a single banner demonstrates strategic foresight and leadership that is sensitive to the needs of others.

For social justice and empowerment movements, Deborah's narrative provides a spiritual framework that underscores themes of liberation and resistance. Within the wider framework of biblical theology, her story highlights the significance of obedient adherence to divine direction as a necessary component for the transformation of society and the redemption of the nation.

Even while the historical accuracy of incidents in the tale of Deborah may be challenged, the narrative's underlying themes and symbolic significance continue to be of utmost importance. It is possible that future investigations will delve more profoundly into the linguistic and creative dimensions of her song to extract newer interpretations of her contribution to the biblical literature (Webb, 2012). In addition, developments in archaeological and historical research have the potential to provide a clearer picture of the social and political landscape of ancient Canaan, which would shed new light on the time of Deborah.

Additionally, additional research could investigate the depiction of Deborah in various cultural and religious traditions, so examining how her narrative has been reinterpreted and understood in a variety of historical contexts. While societal discussions around gender and leadership continue to shift, Deborah's story will probably continue to serve as a key reference point, providing both inspiration and insight into the unchanging topics of faith, leadership, and courage.

The narrative of Deborah in the Hebrew Bible offers a new perspective on leadership by emphasizing the importance of women as key actors in the religious and social-political historical contexts of the past. Her leadership model, which is characterized by wisdom, courage, and collaborative strength, is presented as a challenge to the established ideas of gender restrictions and limitations on leadership. Deborah's legacy transcends her own era, continuing to have an impact on religious thought and contemporary debates regarding leadership and gender equality. Her legacy as a historical figure and as a symbol extends beyond her own time. By viewing things through the lens of her narrative, we can develop a deeper understanding of the complex interactions that occur between faith, leadership, and social change movements.

According to the depiction of Deborah in the Book of Judges, she was a central figure of leadership and inspiration within the community of ancient Israelites. She is a wonderful example of the tremendous influence that women had in shaping the socio-political environment of their time because of the roles that she played as a judge and prophetess. Her legacy continues to be present in current discussions around women's leadership and empowerment, where she argues that gender should not be seen as a barrier to one's ability to influence and lead others. Deborah's tale serves to challenge the stereotypes that have been held in the past and present, reminding us of the significant contributions that women have made throughout history.

# THE LEGACY OF RUTH: A BIBLICAL ARCHETYPE OF LOYALTY AND FRIENDSHIP

But Ruth replied, "Don't urge me to leave you or to turn back from you. Where you go I will go, and where you stay I will stay. Your people will be my people and your God my God. (Ruth 1:16)

In the Hebrew Bible, the story of Ruth is a wonderful story that revolves around themes of devotion, perseverance, and divine providence. Not only did she become the great-grandmother of King David, which established her as a significant ancestral figure in the Judeo-Christian tradition, but the narrative of her life also exemplifies the values of love and companionship. This chapter delves into these topics, analysing the historical and cultural context of Ruth, the influence she had on the tradition of the Bible, and the enduring legacy that she has left behind. It is hoped that the discussion will elucidate Ruth's narrative from several different perspectives and bring attention to its significance in relation to modern situations. The values of friendship and loyalty, which are fundamental to the biblical story and its interpretations throughout history, are reflected in Ruth's words and actions, which serve to underscore how they reflect the values of to the story. It is highlighted how transformative these values are in the formation of resilient relationships and communities by Ruth's uncompromising dedication to Naomi and her willingness to accept a new identity.

According to Miller and Hayes (2008), Ruth's narrative is set in the Iron Age, a time characterized by tribal cultures, in what is now the Middle East. Ruth's story begins with her marriage to Mahlon, an Israelite, in a time when intermarriages were frequently viewed with suspicion owing to the differences in religion and ethnicity. This marriage takes place at the beginning of Ruth's narrative. After the passing of her husband, Ruth was confronted with a dilemma of great importance: whether to go back to her hometown of Moab or to remain with her mother-in-law Naomi, who was an Israelite.

Ruth's statement, "Whither thou goest, I will go," which is recorded in Ruth 1:16, reflects her steadfast devotion to Naomi and her readiness to accept a new life in Bethlehem, which is Naomi's native country. By making this decision, she not only shown her own religious commitment but also demonstrated her respect for the beliefs and people of Naomi, thus bridging the gaps that existed between their cultures and religions. When seen from a historical perspective, this decision highlights Ruth's position as a promoter of unity in times of cultural turmoil, demonstrating her strength in the face of challenge.

There are several key reasons why Ruth's inclusion in the biblical canon a noteworthy development was. According to Landy (2010), the Book of Ruth is one of the few books of the Bible that is focused on a female protagonist, providing a novel perspective on the experiences of women during the time that it was written. Loyalty to one's family, compassion, and unflinching faith are all themes that are highlighted in her narrative. David, who would go on to become one of the most famous kings in Israel, was Ruth's great-grandson, and her actions established the narrative groundwork for him.

It is an act of divine providence that Ruth was devoted to Naomi and later married to Boaz, who was related to Naomi. In addition to guaranteeing the continuation of Naomi's family line, it also ensured that Ruth would be included in the lineage of David and, subsequently, in the lineage of Jesus Christ according to Christian theology. In reference to the ancient understanding of divine intervention and God's overarching purposes, this genealogical inclusion speaks to the divine intervention itself. Through her transformation from an outsider to a key player in God's redemptive narrative, Ruth illustrates the all-encompassing quality of divine grace.

The dedication that Ruth showed to accompany Naomi back to Bethlehem sheds light on the fundamental aspect of companionship in human relationships. Ruth selects loyalty over convenience, despite the difficulties posed by poverty and the uncertainty of life in a foreign country. Not only do her well-known remarks represent a deep relationship between her and Naomi, but they also serve as a reflection of a commitment to the human experience that is common to all. Although she was motivated by love and solidarity, an analysis of Ruth 1:16 demonstrates her willingness to embrace an unpredictable future. This demonstration of loyalty makes a challenge to the dominant socio-cultural standards of the time, bringing to light the ways in which companionship can serve as a radical force in times of crisis.

Not only do Ruth's actions serve as a model of unwavering devotion, but they also serve to empower those who are marginalized within the stories of the Bible. In addition to being a Moabite woman, she challenges ethnic boundaries and demonstrates how loyalty may transcend cultural divides. Ruth demonstrates her willingness to seek for sustenance for herself and Naomi by gleaning in the fields. This action challenges the conventions that portray women in passive roles. Her devotion to Naomi not only serves as a catalyst for her own empowerment, but it also paves the way for her eventual integration into the Israelite community. In the end, it elevates her to the position of a significant ancestor of King David, hence changing the course of events in biblical history. The dynamics of her character are a reaffirmation of the narrative's argument that fidelity may result in empowerment and contributions to society.

The story of Ruth has evolved into a timeless model of faith and friendship, transcending the historical circumstances in which it was originally set. In religious communities, her narrative is often used as an example of exemplary behaviour and loyalty. Ruth's transformation into Judaism and her important role in Jewish culture are two of the reasons why the Book of Ruth is commonly read during the Jewish holiday of Shavuot. Her ancestry is mentioned in the Gospel of Matthew, which highlights her significance in Christ's lineage according to the teachings of Christianity.

The story of Ruth is intertwined with the theme of divine providence, which is highlighted by the fact that Ruth's devotion to God helps to ensure that God's purpose for the line of Israel is carried out. In the words of Barton (2002), Ruth's marriage to Boaz, who was a kinsman-redeemer, is an important event that symbolizes God's grace and the miraculous care that God provides. Within the framework of the biblical narrative tradition, she is portrayed as a pivotal character owing to her connection to King David and her incorporation into the Israelite community. The legacy of Ruth reinforces the idea that acts of devotion and companionship are not only cherished on a personal level, but they are also essential to the realization of divine purpose. This illustrates how individual deeds may reverberate throughout history and influence collective identities.

In current debates, Ruth is frequently utilized as a representation of both acceptance and inclusivity. Her incorporation into Israelite society challenges current ideas of societal limits and xenophobia, advocating for a more comprehensive understanding of community. In addition to providing a biblical framework for compassion and unity, Ruth's fearless crossing of cultural boundaries to support her family is relevant to the present day's global difficulties of migration and cultural integration.

It is also possible to interpret Ruth's declaration of devotion through the perspective of women's empowerment and agency respectively. In Trible's (1978) definition of traditional gender roles, she argues that women can make important life decisions in an era when their roles were mostly domestic. Her assertiveness in choosing her own path is a departure from traditional gender roles. Current feminist interpretations of Ruth's narrative highlight her independence and ability to make difficult choices, providing women with a present-day empowering story.

From a variety of academic standpoints, Ruth's story has been analysed and interpreted. The comprehensive narrative structure and linguistic aspects of the book have been emphasized by literary scholars who have examined its formal qualities. According to Berlin (2005), the poetic conversations that take place between Ruth and Naomi are famous for their emotional depth and rhetorical force, as they offer insight into the interpersonal dynamics that are depicted in the text. Readers can connect with the themes of the story on many different levels because of the style that is concise but expressive.

The account of Ruth is seen by theological scholars as an illustration of God's providence and faithfulness, which is revealed through the activities of human beings. According to this point of view, Ruth's life is a testament to the fact that ordinary individuals have the potential to make extraordinary contributions to the history of divine salvation. From a theological standpoint, Ruth's willingness to convert to a foreign religion, together with the favourable results of her activities, illuminates the transformational power of faith (Williamson, 1985).

When viewed from the lens of historical criticism, the origin of the story provides significant insights into the development of Israelite society and religion. In their research, scholars have looked at Ruth's status as a Moabite, delving into the relationships that ancient Israel had with its neighbouring countries and the gradual development of the Israelite religion to encompass people from other countries. The adoption of this contextual strategy highlights the inclusive theological expansions that took place throughout the biblical era.

The story of Ruth remains an important text in both the academic sphere and the practice of religion. During the ongoing challenges that contemporary society faces regarding integration, identity, and migration, Ruth's narrative serves as a source of hope and enlightenment. The fact that she travelled across different cultures and religions indicates a future in which the integration and acceptance of diverse groups will be of utmost importance.

Ruth's story inspires ongoing reflection in theological circles regarding the question of faith and inclusion and what their nature is. Considering the growing diversity of religious communities, Ruth's narrative may provide a model for enhancing communication and relationship-building between individuals of different faith traditions. The development of a global sense of religious harmony requires this element, which involves constructing bridges rather than raising barriers.

Further academic research on Ruth might delve more deeply into her role as a progenitor within the framework of biblical genealogies. This research would shed light on her significance across a variety of canonical interpretations and within a variety of religious traditions. In addition, feminist interpretations of her story are ready to change, which will provide more profound insights into the agency of women in the Bible and the larger ramifications of their narratives.

Within the realm of literature and artistic activities, Ruth's narrative has served as a source of inspiration for an infinite number of adaptations and interpretations. It is through these creative expressions that Ruth's legacy will continue to exist, perpetually augmenting cultural and artistic endeavours for future generations. In this sense, the narrative of Ruth continues to be not just a treasured religious book but also a vibrant wellspring of motivation and contemplation.

It is a perpetual testament to the strength of faith, love, and moral determination that Ruth's story serves as. As she transforms from a Moabite widow to a matriarch in David's line, her story highlights issues such as fidelity, cultural integration, and the significance of theology. Ruth is a role model for the power that can be found in friendship and the ability that friendship must bridge divides, whether those divides are cultural, religious, or personal. This is true both in the historical context and in the contemporary interpretation. The narrative of her journey, which is summed up in the simple statement, "Whither thou goest, I will go," is a celebration of steadfast devotion and the transformative force of partnership. It provides a light that is relevant to the common spiritual journey taken by humanity.

It is illustrative of how these values can transcends societal boundaries and affect generations. Ruth's narrative is a powerful reminder of the strength of human relationships that are formed on loyalty and love. In both historical and contemporary discussions of friendship and loyalty, Ruth's journey exemplifies how profound relationships can result in divine outcomes. This reinforces the timeless relevance of her character and the values she embodies. As Ruth becomes an important figure in the lineage of King David, her journey serves as a case study in how profound relationships can produce divine results.

# ESTHER: HER COURAGE AND THE SALVATION OF THE JEWISH PEOPLE

For if you remain silent at this time, relief and deliverance for the Jews will arise from another place, but you and your father's family will perish. And who knows but that you have come to your royal position for such a time as this?" (Esther 4:14)

When analysed within the historical framework of the Persian Empire, the story of the Book of Esther, which is included in the Hebrew Bible, is a profound investigation of bravery, identity, and divine providence. The story centres on a young woman who is Jewish and goes by the name of Hadassah, although she is more generally recognized by the name of Esther. She begins in obscurity and works her way up to become the Queen of Persia. An evil guy named Haman was responsible for the plot to exterminate the Jewish people, which serves as the backdrop for the tale that is being told here.

Esther's bravery and strategic acumen in confronting the plot, the cultural and historical complexities of the time, the influence of key characters in the story, various scholarly interpretations, and the enduring legacy of this biblical book will all be discussed in this chapter. In addition, this chapter will go into recent academic discussions regarding the Book of Esther, its significance in the present day, and any future developments that may take place in its study.

In addition to being an interesting story, the Book of Esther explores themes of identity and bravery, as well as the socio-political power dynamics that exist. Esther, who was first known as Hadassah, is the protagonist of this narrative. Her rise to power on the Persian throne presents her with a variety of difficulties and opportunities that are distinctive. The central focus of this chapter is an investigation into the ways in which Esther's dual identity as a Jewish woman and a Persian queen, on the one hand, and her brave acts, on the other hand, combine to create her important role in the prevention of Haman's genocidal plan against the Jewish people. By doing so, the transformation of Hadassah to Esther not only reflects the personal development of Esther but also acts as a catalyst for the survival of the Jewish people, demonstrating the interaction that exists between individual bravery and communal duty.

Esther's narrative takes place in the Persian Empire during the time of King Ahasuerus, who is often recognized as Xerxes I of the years 486 to 465 BCE (Collins, 2018). At this time, the Jewish people were in diaspora, and their fate was uncertain; they were frequently subject to the whims of local authorities. To grasp the seriousness of Esther's deeds and the perilous situation that her people are in, it is essential to have a fundamental understanding of this context.

The Persian Empire was a huge multicultural realm that held a significant position. It was a crossroads where many different cultures and religions converged, which ultimately resulted in a complicated political landscape. Persia was one of the many lands where the Jews found themselves dispersed after they had been exiled from their homeland and had found themselves dispersed across the world.

The central characters in the Story of Esther are the ones who drive the narrative forward. Their actions and motivations are what propel the tale forward. Even though she was not seen as a heroine at first because of her modest background and her secret identity as a Jew, Esther goes on to become a key figure in the liberation of her people. Mordecai, who is Esther's cousin and guardian, is another important figure who embodies the tenacity and faith of the Jewish diaspora through his portrayal. The authority of the empire is represented by a hasuerus, which is portrayed as a strong yet impressionable king. This symbolises the unpredictable character of authority within the empire. Finally, the enemy Haman, who is motivated by a personal grudge and anti-Semitic sentiments, is a personification of the existential threat that the Jewish people face.

The narrative continues to unfold as Esther, upon her accession to the throne, finds herself in a terrible scenario when Mordecai, her uncle, refuses to bow to Haman. This refusal causes Haman to instigate a decree for the extermination of all Jews in the empire. Even though she is hesitant at first, Esther makes the courageous decision to intervene. She urges her people to fast and pray while she gets ready to approach the king without being called, an action that might result in her being put to death (Berlin et al 2014). After Esther reveals her Jewish identity to Ahasuerus and skilfully exposes Haman's scheme, her people are ultimately saved, and Haman is brought down.

Esther's transformation from a passive character to a proactive saviour is an example of bravery in the face of seemingly insurmountable challenges. It is a demonstration of her developing sense of duty and bravery that she would take the risk of approaching the king without an invitation. By doing so, she not only saves her own people but also establishes herself as a significant actor in the history of the Jewish people (Dunn et al,

2005).

Her carefully devised plan to expose Haman is a clear demonstration of her strategic intelligence. Esther creates the ideal scenario for disclosing the danger to her people by hosting two distinct banquets and inviting both the king and Haman. This approach allows her to do so without directly confronting the power structures of the court too soon. Not only does this strategy demonstrate her intellect and foresight, but it also emphasizes the significance of patience and timing when it comes to political manoeuvring.

The combination of Jewish heritage and Persian royal culture is represented by Esther's identity. In the beginning, Esther's concealment of her Jewish identity, as directed by her cousin Mordecai (Esther 2:10), serves to demonstrate her tactical placement in a foreign court. Not only is this concealment an act of self-preservation, but it also serves as an example of the challenges that people in diasporic situations encounter as they navigate numerous identities. To give an example, Esther demonstrates her ability to use her royal influence to protect her people by demonstrating her ability to manoeuvre within the court's politics during the banquet that she is preparing for King Ahasuerus and Haman. The struggle for identity in a society where cultural assimilation is both a strategy for survival and a source of emotional strife is highlighted by this duality, which serves as a key theme in the story.

Esther's bravery shines through as a prominent trait when she makes the audacious decision to approach the king without being invited, an act that might have resulted in her death, as stated in Esther 4:11. Despite her initial apprehension, her determination grows when she learns about the scheme that Haman is working against her people. Through her well-known statement, "If I perish, I perish" (Esther 4:16), she exemplifies the fundamental aspect of brave leadership, which is the willingness to take one's own risk for the benefit of others. Esther's willingness to openly challenge the king reflects her devotion to her community and her identity. This moment serves as a powerful reminder of the tremendous impact that individual agency can have on the process of transforming society. As a direct result of this, her courage serves as a source of inspiration and motivation for the Jewish community to come together in fasting and prayer. This demonstrates the ripple effect that one person's bravery can have on the collective struggle for survival.

One of the most important aspects of Esther's leadership style is the way she goes about convincing others. By employing a combination of diplomatic skills and strategic acumen, she arranges a succession of banquets that ultimately culminate in the disclosing of Haman's secret plan. It is noteworthy that her deliberate postponement of the revelation of her name makes it possible for the build-up of suspense to take place. This guarantees that when she finally discloses the truth, it will have a profound emotional impact (Esther 7:3). Esther's intelligence and grasp of human psychology are highlighted in this narrative technique, which she uses to construct her strategy to manipulate the emotions of the king. In addition, her ability to inspire Mordecai and the Jewish people to act is an illustration of her function as a unifier in addition to her role as a saviour. Esther's actions can be seen as a model of effective leadership that combines personal sacrifice with communal responsibility, highlighting the significance of strategy in the face of adversity. Esther's actions can be seen as a model of effective leadership.

Scholars have offered a variety of interpretations of the Book of Esther, which reflects the diverse character of the text. Some people take it to be a historical narrative that demonstrates the secret presence and providence of God, even though there is no mention of God that is made explicitly in the text itself (Friedman, 2019). Because of this absence, there has been discussions regarding the book's position within the canon and the serious ramifications its theology would have.

According to another point of view, the book of Esther can be interpreted as a tale of political resistance, illustrating the ways in which a community that is marginalized can manoeuvre within and perhaps subvert prevailing power structures to secure its own existence (Fox, 2010). The strategic application of non-violent resistance and diplomacy is emphasized in this reading.

Esther has also been analysed from the perspective of gender studies, with scholars concentrating on her position as a female leader in a society that is dominated by men. By putting her in the role of saviour, her actions redefine the concept of feminine power and leadership, therefore challenging traditional gender standards (Brenner, 1995).

Recent developments in the discussions surrounding the Book of Esther have extended to include its significance in relation to present-day social and political circumstances. These themes of ethnic identity, survival, and advocacy are in line with continuing discussions around minority rights and resistance against oppression. As an illustration, the Jewish holiday of Purim, which commemorates the events of the book, continues to be a season for contemplating these topics. This is evidence of the continued impact that the narrative has had on Jewish culture and consciousness through the ages.

Esther's story is being investigated by scholars within the framework of current political advocacy. Parallels are being drawn between Esther's approach and contemporary social justice and equity movements. When it comes to understanding and enacting change in the present day, the significance of biblical stories as a source of historical frameworks is brought home by this conclusion.

It is possible that, in the future, research on the Book of Esther will continue to focus on comparative studies, which would involve discovering similarities between the stories of Esther and comparable tales from a variety of cultures and faiths around the world. By shedding light on the text's universal topics, such as justice, identity, and resilience, these kinds of studies have the potential to broaden intercultural understanding.

In addition, it is anticipated that interdisciplinary approaches, which incorporate literary, historical, and theological methodologies, will contribute to a deepening of understanding of the subtleties of the text. Additionally, the use of new technologies and digital humanities tools in textual analysis has the potential to open novel ways of investigating this ancient story through other means.

There are numerous themes that are related to bravery, strategic acumen, and resilience that are presented in the Book of Esther. The dynamic journey that Esther took from anonymity to power not only saved her people, but it also offers a timeless investigation into both identity and tenacity. Esther exemplifies the characteristics that are required to traverse and confront the power dynamics that exist within her society through her strategic planning and decisive action. Her narrative reverberates across the ages, providing not just inspiration but also a critical lens through which to examine current difficulties pertaining to identity and justice.

An in-depth analysis of the historical context, the motivations of the characters, and the various interpretations reveals the intricacy and depth of this biblical novel. The continued exploration and discovery of new aspects of Esther's narrative by scholars ensures that the story's significance in relation to modern social challenges will continue to exist. The lessons that can be learned from Esther's story and the important role she played in the history of the Jewish people serve as a constant reminder of the enduring effectiveness of bravery and conviction in bringing about change and achieving peace.

The Book of Esther is a comprehensive account that delves into themes of identity, bravery, and strategic leadership. The metamorphosis of Esther from Hadassah to a powerful queen is a case study in the difficulties of dealing with two identities in the face of existential challenges. Through her daring confrontations and tactical persuasion, she emphasizes her role as a critical actor in ensuring the safety and continuity of her people. In the end, Esther is a symbol of perseverance, showing that acts of bravery taken by individuals can have a significant influence on the community. Because the lessons that are conveyed through her narrative reverberate strongly within the realms of leadership and identity, Esther is a timeless figure whose legacy continues to motivate acts of courage that are committed to serving others.

# PART 2: WOMEN IN THE NEW TESTAMENT: COURAGE, DEVOTION AND SPIRITUAL INSIGHT

Within the rich fabric of the New Testament, women are shown as important characters whose tales reverberate with similar topics such as bravery, devotion, and spiritual insight. The purpose of this book, titled "New Testament Women: Courage, Devotion, and Spiritual Insight," is to shed light on the lives of these extraordinary women, as well as to investigate their distinct contributions to the early Christian movement and their enduring legacy within the faith community.

Throughout the New Testament, there are numerous instances of women who display tremendous faith and resilience in the face of challenges posed by society. Some of these women are Mary, the mother of Jesus, Mary Magdalene, and Priscilla, Wife of Aquila. Both their own experiences and the power of God's grace and strength are reflected in their stories, which serve as powerful testimonies to both God and their own lives. We can gain insight into the significant and revolutionary impact that women had on the early church by analysing their narratives. Additionally, we can draw inspiration from their experiences and provide guidance for present-day believers.

Through this introduction, readers are encouraged to engage with the stories of these women and draw lessons that are applicable to the present day. The stage is set for a more in-depth investigation of the lives of these women. During our exploration of their experiences, we will discover the courage that motivated them to act, the devotion that kept them steadfast in their belief, and the spiritual insights that continue to both challenge and inspire us as we embark on our own journeys of faith. Join us as we honour the extraordinary ladies mentioned in the New Testament and the significant influence they have had on the Christian religion through their work.

# MARY: THE THEOLOGICAL SIGNIFICANCE OF THE VIRGIN MOTHER IN CHRISTIANITY

And Mary said, "I am the Lord's servant; may your
word to me be fulfilled". (Luke 1:38)

Mary is most widely recognized in the Bible as the mother of Jesus Christ, according to its contents. The conceptions that Christians have about the incarnation are fundamentally based on her depiction as a virgin who was chosen by God to conceive Jesus through the power of the Holy Spirit. This chapter will investigate Mary's function in the Bible, the influence she has had on Christian theology, as well as several different viewpoints regarding the significance she holds.

Not only is Mary portrayed in the New Testament as the mother of Jesus Christ, but she is also portrayed as a symbol of divine grace and obedience, making her a key figure in the Christian religion. The story of Mary's virgin conception has a significant impact on the Christian beliefs that underpin the incarnation of God. Her role as the chosen vessel for the incarnation provides an opportunity to gain insight into God's purpose and the essence of holiness. This role establishes a theological framework that is both intricate and nuanced. Additionally, the argument is made in this chapter that

Mary's virginity, as well as her divine selection as the mother of Jesus, not only serve to emphasize her pivotal role in the Christian story of incarnation, but they also reflect deeper theological themes regarding purity, obedience, and the unique relationship that exists between humanity and the divine.

There are only a few references to Mary's character in other books of the New Testament, and she is primarily developed in the Gospels of Matthew and Luke. The Gospel of Matthew provides a depiction of Mary from the point of view of Joseph, highlighting Joseph's difficulty in comprehending Mary's pregnancy and the divine intervention that confirms Mary's position (Matthew 1:18-25). On the other hand, the Gospel of Luke provides a more in-depth description of Mary's experiences, which include the Annunciation, her journey to Elizabeth, and the Magnificat (Luke 1:26-56). Through these passages, Mary is shown to be faithful, obedient, and humble in her acceptance of God's plan for her life.

In Mary's narrative, the Annunciation is a crucial turning point. Mary receives a visit from the angel Gabriel, who informs her that she will become pregnant with a child through the Holy Spirit. Gabriel also tells her that her son will be named Jesus and that he will be the Son of the Highest (Luke 1:31-33). Mary's initial reaction is one of confusion and questioning, as she asks, "How will this be since I am a virgin?" (Luke 1:34). Gabriel explains the divine power that will allow her to conceive, assuring her that "nothing is impossible with God" (Luke 1:37). Mary's response, "I am the Lord's servant; may your word to me be fulfilled" (Luke 1:38), reflects her deep faith and willingness to cooperate with God's purpose.

A further confirmation of Mary's role is provided by her visit to her relative Elizabeth, who is pregnant. Mary's response is the Magnificat, a hymn of praise that honours God's faithfulness and justice (Luke 1:46-55). Elizabeth, who is filled with the Holy Spirit, acknowledges Mary as the mother of the Lord and bestows a blessing upon her (Luke 1:42-45). Mary's understanding of God's preferential preference for the marginalized and poor is reflected in the Magnificat, which is a theme that runs throughout the Gospel of Luke.

The narratives of Mary's birth are not the only ones that she plays. During important times in Jesus' life, such as his infancy, childhood, and ministry, she is there to see him. According to the Gospels, Mary was present at the wedding in Cana, where Jesus performed his first miracle at her request. This event is recorded in John 2:1-12. Additionally, she is there at the crucifixion, when Jesus entrusts her into the care of the apostle John, as recorded in John 19:25-27. Mary's constant presence and support in the life and ministry of Jesus is demonstrated by these examples.

The Incarnation and salvation are two of the most important Christian teachings, and Mary's role as the mother of Jesus has significant theological implications for both doctrines. The concept of the Incarnation, which holds that God took on the form of Jesus Christ, is a fundamental component of the Christian faith. As an integral part of the divine act of conceiving and bearing Jesus, Mary is an important participant in this act. Many Christians hold the belief that Mary's virginity before, throughout, and after the birth of Jesus Christ is a symbol of the holiness and purity that surrounds the conception of Jesus Christ.

There is a different interpretation of Mary's role among the different Christian faiths. In the Catholic faith, Mary is honoured as the Mother of God (Theotokos) and as the Sovereign of the Heavenly Realm. The Catholic faith places a strong emphasis on two important doctrines relating to Mary: the first is the Immaculate Conception, which is the belief that Mary was conceived without the influence of original sin; the second is the Assumption, which is the belief that Mary was taken bodily into heaven at the conclusion of her life on earth. Although these beliefs are not directly mentioned in the Bible, they are formed on interpretations of Scripture as well as historical and theological traditions.

Icons and prayers are used by Eastern Orthodox Christians to honour Mary, referring to her as the Theotokos and expressing their high regard for her through these practices. Within the context of traditional theology, Mary is portrayed as the mediator between God and humanity, the one through whom God took on the form of a human person.

Mary is generally regarded with respect by Protestant denominations; however, her role is not stressed to the same extent as it is by Catholics and Orthodox Christians of the same faith. Mary's role as a faithful servant of God is the primary focus of Protestant theology, which generally rejects the teachings of the Immaculate Conception and the Assumption. Protestantism's founder, Martin Luther, had a high regard for Mary.

There have been several important people who have contributed to the theological understanding of Mary. Saint Augustine, a significant theologian of the fourth and fifth centuries, wrote extensively on Mary's role in the Incarnation and her importance as a model of faith and obedience. Thomas Aquinas, a theologian of the thirteenth century, developed a systematic theology that included detailed reflections on Mary's virtues and her role in salvation. Aquinas (1274) is an example of this. In the context of modern theology, theologians such as Karl Rahner and Hans Urs von Balthasar have recently investigated the significance of Mary, placing an emphasis on her role as a symbol of hope and liberation, as stated by Rahner (1974).

Theologians who identify as feminists have provided a variety of perspectives on Mary. The conventional depictions of Mary as passive and obedient are criticized by some feminist theologians, who argue that these representations serve to reinforce patriarchal standards. In addition to this, other feminist theologians place an emphasis on Mary's power, bravery, and agency, with reference to her role as a prophet and advocate for those who are disadvantaged (Warner, 2016). The complexity of interpreting Mary's role considering current worries regarding gender and power is reflected in these diverse perspectives, which reflect the complexity of the situation.

It is anticipated that the Mary of the Bible and the Christian tradition will continue to evolve in the years to come. Our understanding of the significance of Mary's significance will continue to be shaped by new archaeological discoveries, theological insights, and cultural perspectives. Our understanding of Mary's place in the history of salvation will be further deepened by the continuing dialogue that takes place between various Christian traditions, as well as by the conversations that take place between faiths.

Mary's contribution to the Bible is both complex and significant in its entirety. It is claimed that she is a courageous prophet, the mother of Jesus Christ, and a humble servant of God. Her narrative continues to serve as a source of inspiration and a challenge to believers today, encouraging them to ponder the significance of faith, obedience, and the Incarnation. The many viewpoints on Mary, ranging from established theological interpretations to current feminist critiques, reflect the lasting significance of her narrative for people of all cultural backgrounds.

Not only does Mary have a historical significance in Christianity, but she also continues to be a living tradition that influences the faith and practices of millions of individuals across the globe. Believers are encouraged to seek a deeper relationship with God and to labour for justice and peace in the world because of the example of faith, hope, and love that she provides.

When Mary is depicted in the Gospels as a young woman who was selected for a significant responsibility, it speaks to modern concerns regarding the empowerment of women. By accepting God's call, she challenges traditional conceptions of power and authority and presents a leadership model that is grounded in humility and service to others.

In addition, Mary's Magnificat is a sermon that serves as a reminder of God's concern for the those who are most vulnerable and marginalized in society. To fulfil the vision that she advocates, society must undergo a radical transformation in which the proud are brought low and the humble are elevated. In a world that is characterized by inequity and wrongdoing, this message continues to be relevant.

The many ways in which Mary's role is understood across various Christian traditions serves as a point of emphasis for the diversity that exists within Christianity. Protestants, on the other hand, do not place as much emphasis on Mary's exceptional position as the Mother of God as Catholics and Orthodox Christians do; rather, they concentrate on her role as a faithful follower of Christ. These several points of view reflect the continual theological disputes that exist over the essence of salvation, the function of the saints, and the authority of the salvation history tradition.

There are many different feminist perspectives on Mary, each of which provides valuable insights into the difficulties and chances that women face within religious traditions. Feminist theologians are contributing to a more comprehensive and empowering understanding of Christianity by reasserting Mary's agency and bringing attention to her prophetic voice.

Within the context of Christian theology, Mary's virginity is an aspect that carries significant weight. The doctrine of the virgin birth is succinctly stated in Isaiah 7:14, which contains a prophecy that says, "Look, the young woman is with child and shall bear a son and shall name him Immanuel". Not only does this prophecy establish her virginity as a miraculous event, but it also establishes it as a symbol of divine purity. It reinforces the belief that God came into humanity in a way that was completely miraculous. To comprehend Mary's unique vocation, it is necessary to first grasp the concept of virginity, which imparts a sense of sanctity that is untouched. The Gospel of Matthew seeks to create an image of Jesus as the flawless representative of God by portraying Mary as a virgin. This is done to emphasize the purity and holiness of the child that Mary is to conceive. The concept of virginity goes beyond mere bodily purity, implying that one is spiritually prepared to carry out God's plan.

To have a better understanding of Mary's importance within Christian theology, it is essential to first grasp her acceptance of her divine role. In Luke 1:38, she said to the angel Gabriel, "Here am I, the servant of the Lord; let it be with me according to your word," which is the response that she gave to the angel Gabriel. Then the angel departed from her. It is a demonstration of her obedience as well as her profound faith. Mary's willingness to submit herself to God's plan currently serves as a model of faithfulness for all believers, and this moment exemplifies her commitment to do so. Mary exemplifies immediate acceptance, which highlights a personal connection with God. In contrast to other figures who resist divine calls, such as Moses or Jonah, Mary embodies divine calls. Not only does this acceptance further her purpose, but it also highlights the significance of human agency in relation to divine plans. By acting as a mother who cares for the incarnate Word, she highlights the distinctive way she actively engages in the divine story, which ultimately results in the incarnation of Jesus Christ.

The dynamics of Mary's relationship with the divine are representative of the intersection that exists between humanity and the divine. According to the Gospel of John, the marriage at Cana is a significant event in which Mary intercedes on behalf of the hosts, therefore demonstrating her role as a mediator (John 2:1–11). In this case, Mary's understanding of the divine authority of Jesus serves to illustrate her distinctive role in the redemptive narrative of the Christian faith. Through this mediatory role, Mary is presented as both a mother and an intercessor, which strengthens the idea that her unique relationship with Christ enables believers to approach God through Mary. In addition, her presence at the crucifixion is a demonstration of her unwavering faith in the face of pain, a fact that strikes a powerful chord within Christian communities as they travel through their own spiritual pathways together. Mary's relationship with Jesus is a deep affirmation of God's desire to communicate and engage with humanity using tangible forms, as expressed by God.

There is a possibility that religious traditions can discover common ground and establish bridges of understanding, as demonstrated by the interfaith dialogue on Mary. The shared reverence that Christians and Muslims have for Mary can serve as a basis for developing more collaboration and mutual respect between the two faiths.

In summary, Mary's involvement in the Bible is fundamental to the Christian convictions regarding the Incarnation and salvation. Her narrative serves as a source of inspiration and challenge for believers even now, encouraging them to ponder the significance of faith, obedience, and the life-altering impact that God's love may have on their lives. The multitude of perspectives on Mary, ranging from conventional theological interpretations to modern feminist critiques, reflect the continuing relevance of her tale for people of all cultural backgrounds.

It is quite possible that the ongoing investigation of Mary in the Bible and Christian tradition will continue to undergo modifications in the future. Our understanding of the significance of Mary's significance will continue to be shaped by new archaeological discoveries, theological insights, and cultural perspectives. Both the ongoing conversation between various Christian traditions and the ongoing conversations between Christians and people of other faiths will serve to further enrich our understanding of Mary's place in the history of salvation.

The figure of Mary is a symbol that extends beyond the confines of religion, representing motherhood, compassion, and hope for millions of people across the world. In times of difficulty, her narrative continues to serve as a source of motivation and solace, serving as a reminder to us of the unshakeable strength of faith and the hope that God's love provides.

An examination of Mary's role in the scriptures provides important insights into the formation of Christian theology and the evolution of religious ideas. Through an analysis of the various adaptations of Mary's narrative, we can develop a more comprehensive understanding of the intricacies and subtleties that underlie the Christian religion.

The present Mary continues to be depicted in a variety of contexts, including popular culture and religious art, as is the case with her contemporaneous portrayal. Both the eternal appeal of her narrative and the continuing fascination with her position as the mother of Jesus Christ are reflected in her continuing presence.

In many cases, the theological debates that surround Mary bring up significant questions regarding the character of God, the connection that exists between God and humanity, and the significance that salvation holds. A discussion of these matters is crucial to developing an understanding of the fundamental convictions of Christianity and the various interpretations and reinterpretations that have been given to those beliefs throughout history.

The feminist viewpoints on Mary challenge established beliefs about gender and power, encouraging us to reconsider the roles and obligations that women have in religious communities. To promoting greater equality and inclusivity within Christianity, these perspectives are necessary.

When it comes to Mary, the interfaith dialogue provides an excellent chance to gain knowledge from other religious traditions and to develop bridges of comprehension. It is possible to promote greater collaboration and mutual respect by exploring the common devotion to Mary that exists between Islam and Christianity.

Mary's position as the mother of Jesus goes beyond her biological role and serves as an example of important theological concepts within Christianity, such as purity, obedience, and the intimate relationship that exists between mankind and the divine. Not only is her virginity a remarkable aspect, but it is also a declaration of the supremacy and divine nature of God. In addition, the paradigm of faith and trust that is encouraged for believers to imitate is emphasized by her acceptance of God's will as well as her roles as an intercessor. In the end, Mary is an important figure within Christianity. She exemplifies the intricacies of divine grace and the power of human agency when it is aligned with God's purpose.

CHRIS DUNN

# ELIZABETH: A PILLAR OF FAITH AND RIGHTEOUSNESS

*In a loud voice she exclaimed: "Blessed are you among women, and blessed is the child you will bear!" (Luke 1:42)*

A wonderful example of faith, righteousness, and divine providence may be found in the portrayal of Elizabeth in the New Testament, and more especially in the Gospel of Luke, which provides a fascinating case study. In addition to being known as the mother of John the Baptist and the wife of Zechariah, the narrative of her life is intertwined with that of Mary, the mother of Jesus. This intertwining brings to light issues such as promise, fulfilment, and the changing force of God's grace. This chapter will investigate the relevance of Elizabeth in the New Testament, with particular emphasis on her righteousness, her role in the narrative of salvation, and her everlasting legacy within the Christian faith.

In the New Testament, Elizabeth, the mother of John the Baptist, is presented as a symbol of faith and virtue. In the Gospel of Luke, Elizabeth is described as not just the spouse of Zechariah, a priest, but also as being closely connected to Mary, the mother of Jesus. This places Elizabeth within the context of the major biblical framework that involves divine intervention and familial connections. In a time of social and spiritual turmoil, her tale serves as a key example of righteous living, illustrating the values of faith, obedience, and the realization of God's promises.

The inherent righteousness of Elizabeth, as depicted in Luke 1:6, lays the foundation for the important part that she will play in the continuing narrative of salvation. According to the passage, both Elizabeth and her husband Zechariah were described as "righteous before God, walking in all the commandments and ordinances of the Lord blameless" (Luke 1:6). Not only does this statement position Elizabeth as a behind-the-scenes player, but it also establishes her as a person who possesses a strong sense of faith and ethical moral principles. In the opinion of academics, righteousness in the context of the New Testament refers to a state of being in right relationship with God, which is defined by obedience to divine law and a sincere commitment to God's will (Wright, 2012). Elizabeth's righteousness is not depicted as a strategy to gain God's favour; rather, it is presented as a demonstration of her devotion to God and her openness to receiving his message.

The beginning of Elizabeth's narrative is marked by a dramatic act of faith in response to a challenge. According to the Gospel of Luke, chapter 1, verse 7, Elizabeth and Zechariah are portrayed as "righteous before God, walking blamelessly in all the commandments and statutes of the Lord." Although they were advanced in age and that Elizabeth was barren, they continued to be devoted (Luke 1:18-20). The culmination of this faith is the announcement of John's birth by the angel Gabriel. This announcement represents not just the realization of their own wish for a kid, but it also signifies the arrival of a momentous person in the history of the Bible (Luke 1:13-17). Elizabeth is a role model for believers because she demonstrates unwavering trust in God's plan, even when situations appear to be impossible. Elizabeth's faith is a model for believers everywhere.

Elizabeth's infertility is an essential component of her narrative since it serves to emphasize the miraculousness of the conception of John the Baptist through the Holy Spirit. In the context of ancient Jewish culture, being unable to have children was frequently interpreted as a sign of either a curse or disfavour from God (Barton & Muddiman, 2007). Inability to conceive would have been a source of social stigma as well as personal anguish for Elizabeth in her situation. On the other hand, her infertility is a canvas on which the power and grace of God are painted in a striking and vivid manner. Zechariah was told by the angel Gabriel that Elizabeth, his wife, would give birth to a son when she was advanced in age. This message is a clear indication that God's purpose surpasses the boundaries that humans impose on themselves (Luke 1:13). In addition to the births of Isaac to Sarah and Samuel to Hannah, this miraculous conception is a repetition of other occurrences in the Old Testament. This repetition reinforces the idea that God frequently selects the unlikable and the disenfranchised to carry out His plans.

Moreover, the story of Elizabeth is inextricably linked to the life of Mary, who was the mother of Jesus according to the Christian faith. Mary goes to see Elizabeth, who welcomes her with a mighty declaration, saying, "Blessed are you among women, and blessed is the fruit of your womb!" (Luke 1:42). Mary learns of her own miraculous conception of Jesus. Through this encounter, Elizabeth demonstrates her recognition of Mary's sacred vocation, thus positioning her as a motherly figure within the New Testament narrative. In addition to highlighting the significance of supportive relationships among women, Elizabeth's reaction indicates that there is a shared mission in bringing forth God's purpose. In demonstrating how God's promises frequently demand the involvement and support of a community, the relationship between Elizabeth and Mary serves to reinforce the theme of community in faith.

The encounter between Elizabeth and Mary, which is commonly referred to as the Visitation, is one of the most emotionally charged and theologically significant events recorded in the Gospel of Luke. When Mary, who is carrying Jesus, goes to see Elizabeth, the baby John jumps in Elizabeth's womb. Elizabeth is also filled with the Holy Spirit, according to Luke 1:41. Even before Jesus was born, this incident is understood to have constituted a recognition of his divine identity by others. The subsequent statement made by Elizabeth, which reads, "Blessed are you among women, and blessed is the fruit of your womb!" serves as a prophetic affirmation of Mary's distinct position as the mother of the Messiah. Theologians believe that Elizabeth's greeting is not only a personal compliment, but rather a God-inspired acknowledgment of Mary and the importance of the kid that she is carrying. (Brown, 1999). A profound understanding of God's plan for salvation and her own position within it is reflected in Elizabeth's words.

John the Baptist, who was the son of Elizabeth, was a key figure in the process of preparing the way for Jesus. In his capacity as the forerunner of the Messiah, John the Baptist was marked by a ministry that consisted of a call to repentance and a proclamation of the coming kingdom of God, as recorded in Matthew 3:1-12. John's birth, which was announced by an angel and verified by miraculous circumstances, served to highlight his unique position as a prophet who had been chosen by God. John the Baptist is seen by biblical scholars as the last of the Old Testament prophets and the first herald of the New Covenant. His role emphasizes the continuity and fulfilment of God's redemptive strategy, as explained by Witherington III (1997). Although the New Testament does not provide a comprehensive description of Elizabeth's impact on John's religious formation, it is possible to deduce such an influence from the fact that she and Zechariah were both upright and devout people who taught John to have a profound respect for God.

The legacy of Elizabeth extends beyond her direct involvement in the New Testament story, influencing Christian theology, art, and devotion practices. Elizabeth is honoured in the Christian tradition as a paragon of faith, humility, and submission to what God has revealed through his creation. It is an inspiration to believers of all ages that she is ready to accept God's plan, even when she is confronted with difficult circumstances and the expectations of society. Elizabeth is said to exemplify the qualities of perseverance, hope, and trust in God's promises, according to several different theologians (Johnson, 2006). The testimony of believers serves as a reminder that God's power is frequently revealed in ways that are not anticipated, and that even when things are tough, God is still able to bring about His plans.

Not only does Elizabeth's life exemplify the spiritual height that she possesses, but it also serves as a model of righteousness in the context of Christian living. Her song of praise, the Magnificat (Luke 1:46-55), which mirrors biblical hymns of thanksgiving, and emphasizes her joyful acceptance of God's will, is a reflection of her spontaneous and humble reaction to the wonderful news of her being a mother. Elizabeth's focus on being humble, being thankful, and recognizing the greatness of God acts as an instruction for those who have faith. In a wider sense, her life challenges modern believers to accept their responsibilities in carrying out divine aims while yet remaining virtuous and obedient, reflecting Elizabeth's example of living a life that is rooted in faith.

When it comes to art, Elizabeth is frequently shown alongside Mary in depictions of the Visitation scene. In addition to emphasizing the topics of divine grace and maternal solidarity, these artistic representations capture the closeness and spiritual significance of their encounter, which is highlighted by the divine grace. Historians of art have noted that in many representations of the Visitation, the focus is placed on the contrast between the younger, pregnant Mary and the older, barren Elizabeth. This contrast serves as a symbol for the intersection of the Old and New Covenants (Hall, 1983). It is through these artistic portrayals that one is reminded visually of Elizabeth's relationship to Mary, the mother of Jesus, and the part that Elizabeth played in the story of salvation.

Elizabeth is honoured in the liturgical calendars of several Christian denominations according to the practice of devotion. The common thread that runs through the various traditions is the acknowledgment of her sanctity and her contribution to the realization of God's purpose, even though her feast day is commemorated on a variety of dates across different traditions. The commemoration of Elizabeth in the church calendar, according to experts in liturgy, provides an occasion for believers to contemplate her model of faith and to request her intercession. During the season of Advent, which is the season of preparation for the celebration of the birth of Christ, believers are frequently reminded of the significance of preparing their hearts to receive God's grace through the reading and preaching of her story.

Current readings of Elizabeth's narrative place a strong emphasis on its applicability to the issues and challenges that are faced in the present day. In a time characterized by social disparity, cultural divides, and spiritual uncertainty, Elizabeth's model of righteousness and compassion provides a vision of hope and transformation that is both convincing and inspiring. The narrative of Elizabeth, according to current theologians, encourages Christians to accept a comprehensive definition of righteousness that includes not only individual ethics but also social justice (Schüssler Fiorenza, 1992). Women who may feel marginalized or undervalued can find inspiration in her willingness to defy societal norms and embrace God's call to motherhood, which serves as an example to them.

In addition, Elizabeth's narrative brings attention to the significance of relationships between different generations and the passing on of faith from one generation to the subsequent one. It is the responsibility of parents and mentors to cultivate a love for God and a dedication to His purposes in young people, as demonstrated by her involvement in the spiritual development of John the Baptist. Education professionals believe that the example set by Elizabeth highlights the need of developing supportive and nurturing settings in which young people may develop their faith and uncover their own unique vocation (Parks, 2005).

Since Elizabeth's narrative is continuing, it is possible that future developments pertaining to her tale would result in the further exploration of her character in theological scholarship, creative artistic expressions, and religious activities. As scholars continue to acquire new understandings of the historical and cultural context of the New Testament, they may provide additional light on the significance and role that Elizabeth played. It is possible for artists to continue producing new and original representations of Elizabeth and Mary, while simultaneously reflecting the eternal values of faith, hope, and love. It is possible that devotional writers will continue to take inspiration from the example set by Elizabeth, offering a variety of new perspectives on how her narrative can be used to enlighten and enhance the spiritual lives of believers.

The depiction of Elizabeth in the New Testament is a testimony to the transformative power of faith and the infinite grace that God bestows upon those who believe. Through her righteousness, her extraordinary conception of John the Baptist, and her prophetic encounter with Mary, she has established an enduring legacy as a paradigm of Christian virtue. Her narrative continues to serve as a source of inspiration and challenge for believers, encouraging them to accept God's call, to have faith in His promises, and to live lives that are characterized by righteousness and compassion. Not only does Elizabeth possess notable historical significance, but she also maintains a relevant position throughout the continuing narrative of redemption, which is another aspect of her significance. Not only does Elizabeth's story in the New Testament emphasize her significance as the mother of John the Baptist, but it also provides important insights on faith, community, and righteousness. Through her unshakeable faith in God's promises in the face of personal challenges, her spiritual kinship with Mary, and her role as a paradigm of upright living, she exemplifies a deep connection to the fundamental ideas that underpin the New Testament. As present-day readers engage with Elizabeth's narrative, they are encouraged to reflect on their own faith journeys, using her wonderful life of obedience and the realization of God's divine purpose as a source of motivation for their own journeys.

# MARY MAGDALENE: THE DISCIPLE OF JESUS AND THE FIRST WITNESS OF RESURRECTION

Mary Magdalene went to the disciples with the news:
"I have seen the Lord!" And she told them that he
had said these things to her. (John 20:18)

Mary Magdalene is a fascinating person in the New Testament, and she is frequently acknowledged as a key role in the stories that surround the death and resurrection of Jesus Christ. There has been a significant amount of scholarly interest, theological reflection, and artistic representation directed toward the distinctive role that she plays and the contributions that she makes as a follower of Jesus. This chapter will investigate the historical context of Mary Magdalene, analyse the multiple roles she played in the New Testament, and evaluate her influence and legacy in early Christianity and other subsequent eras. A thorough understanding of her significance will be provided, as recent interpretations and current perspectives on Mary Magdalene will also be discussed.

Mary Magdalene is portrayed in the New Testament as a significant follower of Jesus, whose significance goes beyond the fact that she was a disciple who was also a woman. During the most important times in the life of Jesus, she is a significant person. The role of

Mary Magdalene transcends traditional gender norms, which not only demonstrates her significance to the early Christian faith but also challenges those norms. In addition to providing insights into the social and theological dynamics of the early church, her one contribution highlights her important role in the narrative of the resurrection.

In the New Testament, the accounts of Mary Magdalene are short but extremely significant. In the past, it was said that Jesus had healed her, and that he had cast out "seven demons" from her, as recorded in Mark 16:9 and Luke 8:2 of the New Testament. The significance of this healing lies in the fact that it symbolizes her transition from a woman who was tormented by spiritual distress to a devoted lover of Jesus Christ. One of the ways in which Christ's ministry was characterized was that people of all genders and backgrounds were incorporated into his community of followers. Her presence among Jesus' disciples, who were mostly male, is an example of this inclusive aspect. The incorrect identification of Mary Magdalene with the unnamed sinful woman in Luke 7:37-50 led to her being thought of as either a prostitute or a penitent woman from the beginning of time. However, contemporary scholarship generally rejects this confusion, preferring instead to recognize her as a disciple who had a role that was different from the others (Schaberg, 2002).

The journey of Mary Magdalene began with her healing by Jesus, an act that not only transformed her life but also established her relationship with his ministry. In Luke 8:2, she is referred to as someone from whom seven demons were exorcised by Jesus, which is a metaphor for a radical transformation. Not only does her healing represent a physical recovery, but it also signifies her new role as a disciple and supporter of the ministry. During Jesus' ministry, she was constantly portrayed alongside other important people, such as the apostles, and she was unwavering in her devotion. As an illustration, when Jesus was being crucified, there were only a handful of disciples present. Mary Magdalene was one of those disciples, which demonstrates how devoted she was (John 19:25). Not only does her presence during such a critical moment demonstrate her commitment, but it also demonstrates her exceptional position as a woman in a movement that is largely controlled by men. When it comes to religious contexts, women have frequently been excluded from participation, which is a departure from traditional gender roles that is shown in this devotion.

The fact that Mary Magdalene was present at key moments in the life of Jesus underscores the significance of her relationship with Jesus. According to Matthew 27:55-56, she is mentioned as one of the women who travelled with Jesus as he went across Galilee and Jerusalem during his various journeys. It is significant that she is shown to be standing close to the cross during the crucifixion of Jesus. This is a demonstration of her dedication and bravery at a period when many of the male disciples had fled. (John 19:25) When considering the presence of women, such as Mary Magdalene, in the accounts of the crucifixion, it is important to rethink the social and gender standards that were prevalent within the early Christian groups (Ehrman, 2012).

According to the Gospel of John, Mary Magdalene was the very first person to see Jesus after he had risen from the dead. This is a role that carries a great deal of significance. She was given the title of "apostle to the apostles" because of her encounter with the risen Christ and the commission she received to tell the apostles about his resurrection (John 20:11-18). Not only does Mary's participation in proclaiming the resurrection serve to lend credibility to the testimony of women in religious contexts, but it also represents a significant theological shift, in which the resurrection, which is the foundation of the Christian faith, was first announced by a woman

(King, 2003). This designation highlights her prominence in the early Church and challenges the conventional ecclesiastical hierarchies that many times barred women from leadership positions.

It is possible that the story of Mary Magdalene seeing Jesus after he has risen from the dead is one of the most interesting aspects of the overall narrative of the resurrection. It is recorded in John 20:14-18 that she has an encounter with the resurrected Christ outside the tomb, which makes her the first person to experience this amazing event (John 20:14-18). Because it highlights her importance in the early stages of Christianity, this moment is an important one. Traditionally, women were restricted in their roles within society, yet Mary Magdalene's experience positions her as a crucial figure in the foundational moments of the Christian faith. The directive given by Jesus to Mary, asking her to inform the disciples of his resurrection, also places her in an apostolic role, as she becomes the bearer of the vital news of the resurrection (Matthew 28:10). This aspect of her story challenges the patriarchal narratives prevalent in the culture of her time, establishing her as a bridge between the divine and the community of believers.

In exploring the historical context of Mary Magdalene, it is crucial to understand the socio-cultural milieu of first-century Palestine. Jewish society during this period was predominantly patriarchal, with limited roles for women within religious domains. However, the Synoptic Gospels portray women as active participants in Jesus' ministry, challenging predominant gender roles and foreshadowing the more egalitarian ethic that would emerge in Christian doctrine. Mary Magdalene exemplifies this shift as an empowered disciple who transcends societal limitations to emerge as a central figure in the Christian narrative (Brock & Thistlethwaite, 1996).

Mary Magdalene's role extends beyond that of a follower; she embodies the complexities of women in the early church. Her post-resurrection mission of spreading the news of Jesus' resurrection poses significant implications for understanding leadership dynamics within early Christianity. The early Christians often faced oppression and persecution, making the role of female figures like Mary vital for fostering resilience and hope. In addition, her story has been interpreted in several different contexts, which further emphasizes the need for present-day readers and church leaders to reconsider the contributions that women have made in their local communities. Experts in the field argue that her testimony lends more credibility to the narrative of the resurrection because she was originally marginalized by society. These kinds of conversations help to clarify the necessity of acknowledging and reconciling the historical gender prejudices that have been used to underline the achievements of female leaders, as well as the need of expanding the understanding of Christian tradition.

Over the course of many centuries, the figure of Mary Magdalene has been both interpreted and reinterpreted, serving as an icon of a variety of theological and cultural currents throughout history. In the sixth century, early church authorities such as Pope Gregory the Great established her identity as a repented sinner by merging her story with that of other female characters. This portrayal continued to exist well into the Middle Ages and had a significant impact on much of the art and literature produced in the Western world. In contrast to this, the apocryphal writings, such as the Gospel of Mary, present her as a venerated teacher and spiritual guide. She is frequently depicted as conflicting with the apostle Peter, which reflects early intra-Christian disagreements regarding authority and orthodoxy.

Mary Magdalene's legacy has been recovered and re-evaluated with the help of contemporary scholarship and feminist theology, both of which have played important roles. The contribution that she made to ecclesiastical history is being challenged by present theologians, who argue for a re-evaluation of her work based on historical textual analysis and context. For instance, Elaine Pagels and Karen King place an emphasis on her role as a spiritual leader and interlocutor with Jesus, so portraying her as an advocate for a more inclusive and varied knowledge of the dynamics of the early church (Pagels & King, 2008).

In addition, the rediscovery of apocryphal gospels and the research that followed have served to enrich the discussion that surrounds Mary Magdalene. The Gospel of Mary, which was found in the late 19th century, presents a different story that depicts her as having profound theological insights and understanding that are only surpassed by those of Jesus himself. According to Meyer and De Boer (2004), these writings highlight the diversity of early Christian thought and imply that Mary Magdalene's position as a leader was perhaps more pervasive in early Christian groups than had been previously acknowledged.

The influence that Mary Magdalene had on culture and religion continues to be felt in the present day. Through her example, several different Christian denominations are motivated to pursue a more equitable representation of women in ecclesiastical leadership positions. Her pivotal role in the resurrection tale has served as a source of inspiration for certain progressive strands of Christianity, which have utilized her example to advocate for the ordination of women. The reconceptualization of her function is indicative of larger societal endeavours to acknowledge the contributions that women make in a variety of fields and to question the patriarchal structures that exist within religious organizations.

There has been a further broadening of the interpretations of Mary Magdalene by popular culture over the past few decades. Her life and legacy are still being explored in films, books, and academic publications, all of which strive to strike a balance between the accuracy of the historical record and the inventiveness of the storytelling. The continuing fascination with the character of Mary Magdalene is demonstrated by the renewed public interest and debate that was sparked by Dan Brown's "The Da Vinci Code," which is a significant modern representation of her character. Even though Brown's work is made up, it brings up important questions regarding the historical depiction of Mary and the ways in which her portrayal influences contemporary understandings of gender and spirituality (Brown, 2003).

Considering the future, Mary Magdalene's legacy provides an opportunity to reflect on the continuing path toward gender equality within the contexts of religious practice. In her capacity as a pioneer, she encourages us to reconsider established stories and to recognize the many different voices that have contributed to the formation of the history of religion. Additionally, the ongoing scholarly interest in Mary Magdalene exemplifies the significance of interdisciplinary methods in demonstrating the vast intricacy that is inherent in historical characters. Our understanding of Mary Magdalene's position in history and theology will very likely be updated and refined as new archaeological discoveries and textual analyses come to light. Additionally, these new discoveries will shed light on the extraordinary contributions that she made (Schaberg, 2004).

The presence and influence of Mary Magdalene in the New Testament story provide a tremendous foundation that continues to be a source of inspiration and invites reinterpretation. The journey that she made, from a disturbed person in search of healing to a respected disciple and the first witness to the resurrection, embodies elements of redemption, empowerment, and metamorphosis. We can gain insight into the complexities of early Christianity and the changing positions of women within religious spheres through the examination of her life and legacy. As a result, the study of Mary Magdalene is not only an inquiry into a historical person but also a more comprehensive reflection on identity, authority, and the ongoing quest for truth and equality across both temporal and spiritual domains.

Mary Magdalene's significant impact on early Christianity is shown by her role as a disciple and her role as the first witness of the resurrection of Jesus Christ. Mary Magdalene is a role model for the significant contributions that women made to the early church because she challenged conventional gender roles. She is a testimony to the important contributions that women made to the early church. Ultimately, she was able to amplify the message of hope and resurrection. The healing that Jesus performed on her marks the beginning of her incredible path, during which she not only supported him throughout his ministry but also played a critical role after his resurrection. Her legacy necessitates a re-evaluation of the roles that women have played in Christianity and emphasizes the significance of inclusivity in religious narratives as contemporary debates around gender dynamics continue.

# ANNA THE PROPHETESS: A LIFELONG DEVOTION AND RECOGNITION OF THE MESSIAH

*Coming up to them at that very moment, she gave thanks to God and spoke about the child to all who were looking forward to the redemption of Jerusalem. (Luke 2:38)*

This chapter investigates the role of Anna the Prophetess in the New Testament, with a focus on her devotion, prophetic gift, and her identification of Jesus as the Messiah. During the analysis, her significance within the historical and theological context of the time will be emphasized, with particular attention paid to her lasting impact on Christian tradition.

Within the context of the New Testament story, Anna, a character who is only briefly mentioned in Luke 2:36-38, is a representation of unwavering faith and prophetic discernment. Considering her presence in the Temple, her commitment to prayer and fasting, and her acknowledgment of the infant Jesus as the Messiah who was prophesied, she provides a wonderful tapestry for theological reflection. The purpose of this chapter is to delve into the significance of Anna, exploring her role within the historical and religious context of first-century Judaism, examining the nature of her prophetic gift, and considering her enduring impact on Christian understandings of devotion, expectation, and the revelation of Jesus Christ.

During Jesus' presentation in the Temple, she had an encounter with Jesus, which serves to emphasize her role as a prophetic figure. This encounter demonstrates her remarkable ability to recognize the significance of Jesus as the Messiah who was foretold. In this case, Anna the Prophetess is presented as a paradigm of unflinching faith and devotion in the New Testament. This assertion highlights the significance of spiritual discernment and the recognition of divine truth, which is exemplified by Anna's dedication to worshiping in the Temple and her prophetic identification of Jesus as the Messiah.

To comprehend the importance of Anna, it is necessary to consider the world in which she resided. In the first century, Palestine was a community that was deeply immersed in religious fervour and anticipation for a Messiah. In the context of Roman rule, the Jewish people yearned for the realization of ancient prophecies that foretold the coming of a deliverer who would restore the glory of Israel (Horsley, 2003). According to Evans (2013), the Temple in Jerusalem was the focal point of the religious activities of the Jewish people, where they would gather for pilgrimage, offer sacrifices, and pray. Within this context, different people and organizations had different understandings of the scripture and varying degrees of anticipation for the coming of the Messiah. These different ways of thinking are reflected in the Gospels themselves, which depict characters such as John the Baptist, the wise men from the East, and Anna the Prophetess, among others, as individuals who are sensitive to the signs of the times and open to the unfolding revelation of God's plan (Brown, 2016).

The Gospel of Luke places a strong emphasis on the involvement of women in the story of Jesus' life and ministry. In his portrayal of women as active participants in God's redemptive plan, he emphasizes those who have been frequently neglected by society. According to Gaventa (1999), Mary, the mother of Jesus, Elizabeth, the mother of John the Baptist, and other women disciples are presented as archetypes of faith, obedience, and prophetic discernment. Anna is a perfect example of this pattern. Anna is depicted as a lady of great piety and devotion, and she is referred to as a prophetess, a title that signifies divine inspiration and the capacity to communicate the word of God. In addition to her advanced age, her extended period of widowhood, and her frequent presence in the Temple, where she was involved in worship, fasting, and prayer, all these factors emphasize her unshakable dedication to God (Witherington III, 2001).

In terms of Anna, the information that is given in the Gospel of Luke is of utmost importance. According to Levine & Knight (2006), her tribal affiliation, which identifies her as a member of the Asher tribe, one of the so-called "lost tribes" of Israel, indicates that she has a relationship to the hope that all of Israel would be restored. Her age, which is "very old," as well as her status as a widow of numerous years, illustrate her life of perseverance and faithfulness in the face of adversity (Schafer, 2009). Her profound commitment to God and her unshakable hope for the realization of God's promises is demonstrated by her constant presence in the Temple, where she "worshipping with fasting and prayer night and day" (Green, 1997).

When Jesus is taken by his parents to the Temple for the regular purification ceremonies, that is the moment that marks the turning point in Anna's tale. According to Luke, Anna identified the new-born Jesus as the Messiah "coming up at that very hour," which means she recognized him. According to Stein (1992), the phrase "at that very hour" connotes divine timing, which suggests that Anna's presence in the Temple was heavenly planned to coincide with the arrival of the Messiah. It is not simply through observation that she recognizes Jesus; rather, it is through prophetic insight that she does so. In accordance with Luke 2:38, she "gave thanks to God and spoke of him to all who were waiting for the redemption of Jerusalem." By participating in this act of thanksgiving and proclamation, she reaffirms her position as a witness to the Messiah, spreading the message of salvation to others who shared her desire for Israel's deliverance.

The text does not provide a clear definition of the character of Anna's prophetic gift. It is possible that her capacity to identify Jesus as the Messiah is indicative of a profound understanding of scripture, a sensitivity to the guidance of the Holy Spirit, and a close relationship with God that has been developed through years of prayer and fasting (Keener, 2014). According to Barton (1986), prophecy in the Old Testament involved a variety of activities, such as forthtelling, which was the act of proclaiming God's word to the current generation, and foretelling, which was the act of predicting forthcoming events. It is fair to assume that Anna's prophetic gift included a deeper understanding of God's plans and a capacity to discern the signs of the times, even though the primary focus of her prophecy was on identifying and declaring the identity of Jesus.

There are several reasons why Anna's identification of Jesus as the Messiah is an important event. To begin, it verifies Jesus' identity as the deliverer who was foretold, which is consistent with the prophecies that were made in the Old Testament and the hopes that were held by a significant number of Jewish people (Wright, 2015). Second, it emphasizes the significance of spiritual discernment and the capacity to identify God's presence in ways that are not always anticipated or recognized. Many others, including religious leaders, were blind to the presence of the Messiah, even though Anna, an elderly widow, recognized the Messiah in an infant (Bock, 1994).

In addition, it emphasizes the universality of God's redemptive plan, which includes people of all ages, both men and women, and individuals from every tribe and background. The fact that Anna was included in the Gospel of Luke is evidence that God's grace is accessible to all those who strive to find him with an honest heart.

Anna the Prophetess is a model of a life that is completely committed to spiritual activities. In the passage from Luke 2:36-37, it is stated that she devoted decades to the Temple, where she served God through the disciplines of prayer and fasting. She illustrated the importance of committed worship in the life of a believer. Not only does Anna's portrayal as a widow highlight her devotion, but it also emphasizes her commitment to God. When she lost her spouse, she did not turn to worldly pleasures; rather, she developed an even greater dedication to serving God. This unyielding devotion puts her in stark contrast to the cultural standards of her day, which dictated that widows were often marginalized and that they were expected to find a new spouse. Anna's role as a spiritual leader is highlighted by her full-time commitment to worship, which is not influenced by any social norms. In addition, her deep longing for communion with God is expressed through the practice of fasting, which serves as both a form of sacrifice and a spiritual discipline. When she is presented with Jesus as the Messiah, her lifestyle provides her with prophetic insight, which is a vital quality that allows her to recognize Jesus as the Messiah when he is presented.

Not only does Anna's encounter with Jesus constitute a significant occasion for her, but it also constitutes a pivotal moment in the overarching story of the New Testament. Her declaration acts as a very powerful testimony of faith since she recognizes Jesus as the Messiah when he is first presented to her. As stated in Luke 2:38, Anna 'spoke about the child to all who were looking forward to the redemption of Jerusalem,' which is what she did. Not only does this prophetic recognition reflect her own personal faith, but it also acts as a communal call to others who are waiting for salvation to join her. Anna's acknowledgment of Jesus demonstrates her deep understanding of the Messianic hopes that are prevalent in Jewish tradition, which is evidence that her many years of prayer and worship provided her with a spirit of discernment. There are those who believe that Anna embodies the continuity of the prophetic tradition in Israel because she occupies a position that has traditionally been held by male prophets. This is a significant bridge that has been missing in the historical account. Her prophetic voice represents a key moment that assures believers that God's promises are continuing to be fulfilled throughout the present time.

Anna's narrative has struck a chord with Christians throughout history, inspiring a significant number of individuals to commit their lives to prayer, witnessing, and acts of devotion. Women have frequently considered her to be a role model of female leadership and prophetic ministry, making her example particularly relevant for them. As heirs to Anna's legacy of prophetic insight and steadfast faith, one can look to figures such as Hildegard of Bingen, Julian of Norwich, and Catherine of Siena, all of whom were women who exercised significant spiritual influence within the Church. In the context of modern Christianity, Anna's narrative continues to serve as a source of motivation for women to accept their unique talents and to actively participate in the life and ministry of the Church.

Not only does Anna the Prophetess have a legacy that extends beyond her direct relationships with Jesus, but she also reverberates throughout Christian teachings as a symbol of faithfulness and devotion. Believers who are seeking for spiritual depth can look to her life, which is characterized by perseverance in worship and a deep relationship with God, as a model to follow. Within the framework of her character, the theological implications of her character highlight the significance of unwavering prayer and community articulation in recognizing divine realities. In a sense, Anna's role is not limited to the past; rather, her example provides a foundation for a contemporary understanding of prophetic witnesses and highlights the significance of maintaining spiritual vigilance. Her pronouncement acts as a catalyst, inspiring people to continually engage with the message of Jesus and bringing to light the importance of women in the prophetic tradition. In the context of the continuing discussions that surround the roles that women play in faith groups, Anna is a prominent figure whose existence raises questions about the inclusivity of spiritual gifts and the various ways in which God conveys divine truths.

In addition, Anna's narrative serves as a reminder of the significance of having faith that spans multiple generations. Older generations play an important role in transmitting the faith to younger generations, as evidenced by her advanced age and her presence in the Temple with Simeon, another elderly person who identified Jesus as the Messiah (Campolo, 2005). In a culture that frequently excludes older people, Anna sets an example for us by encouraging us to appreciate the knowledge and experience of senior individuals and to acknowledge the significant contribution that they make to the spiritual development of both individuals and communities.

It is quite likely that the narrative of Anna the Prophetess will continue to serve as a source of inspiration and challenge for Christians in a variety of ways in the future. During its struggle with problems such as gender equality, social justice, and intergenerational relationships, the Church is presented with a powerful reminder of the necessity of valuing the contributions of all members of the community, regardless of their age, gender, or origin, by the example set by Anna. All who aspire to follow Christ and to be involved in the development of God's redemptive purpose can look to her as a model because of her unflinching faith, her prophetic insight, and her commitment to prayer and worship.

When it comes to the New Testament, Anna the Prophetess is a wonderful illustration of unshakable faith, commitment, and spiritual discernment. Her life is a living example of what it means to be devoted to God, which is defined by unchanging worship and prayer, which ultimately results in her being recognized by God as the Messiah along with Jesus. A deeper understanding of the roles that women have had in religious traditions may be gained by recognizing the contributions that Anna has made, which reveals the significant influence that prophetic figures have had on communal faith narratives. Not only does Anna the Prophetess serve to enhance the biblical text, but she also continues to serve as a source of inspiration for believers, encouraging them to seek out spiritual fulfilment and prophetic truth in their lives today.

Anna the Prophetess is a remarkable character in the New Testament. She is a testimony to the unshakeable faith, prophetic insight, and life-changing power that comes from meeting the Messiah. Even though it is short, her tale presents a rich tapestry for theological reflection, which has served as a source of inspiration for Christians throughout history to live lives of devotion, witness, and hope. We can gain a deeper understanding of the importance of this extraordinary lady and the eternal message that her tale conveys by analysing her role within the historical and theological context of first-century Judaism, investigating the nature of her prophetic gift, and considering the lasting influence that she has had on Christian tradition.

# MARTHA OF BETHANY: THE ACTIVE SERVANT IN BIBLICAL HOSPITALITY

"Yes, Lord," she replied, "I believe that you are the Messiah, the Son of God, who is to come into the world." (John 11:27)

In the Christian tradition, Martha is a prominent figure who symbolizes active service and practical devotion. Although she is frequently overshadowed by her sister Mary in biblical tales, she is an important figure. This chapter provides an analysis of the theological ramifications of Martha's service-oriented approach to faith, as portrayed in the Gospels, with a focus on her interactions with Jesus. Martha's character is explored in this chapter. It investigates the historical and cultural context of Martha's conduct, evaluates the effect that her representation has had on Christian thought and practice, and considers several different interpretations of her role in the story.

When it comes to hospitality, Martha is portrayed in the Gospel of Luke as a figure of active service and practical involvement. This stands in stark contrast to her sister Mary, who prefers to sit at the feet of Jesus and focus on spiritual learning. By examining Martha's role in the context of her ministry to Jesus, this chapter investigates the consequences that this has for the understanding of discipleship, particularly the balance that exists between active engagement in service and the necessity of spiritual fulfilment. Through Martha's unwavering commitment to her duties, a strong illustration may be seen of how hospitality can reflect one's faith and devotion to the teachings of Jesus Christ.

In conclusion, the major point of this chapter is that the narrative of Martha provides important insights into the intricacies of faith, service, and the relationship between contemplation and action in the Christian way of life.

The Gospel of Luke (10:38-42) is the book of the Bible that contains the most important manifestation of Martha. In this passage, Jesus goes to Bethany, which is Martha's home. The story illustrates the difference between Martha's active participation in the preparations for the household and Mary's decision to sit at the feet of Jesus and pay attention to what he had to teach.

The tension between action and contemplation is illustrated by Martha's interaction with Mary, according to the narrative. Mary, on the other hand, sits at the feet of Jesus and engages with his teachings, as stated in Luke 10:39. This contrasts with Martha, who is busy with her duties. This contrast serves to highlight the differing approaches to discipleship that are taken; Martha's active involvement is juxtaposed with Mary's contemplative attitude. Jesus' response to Martha, which says, "Martha, Martha, you are worried and upset about many things, but few things are needed or indeed only one" (Luke 10:41-42), encourages Martha to re-evaluate her priorities. It is possible to interpret this moment as a challenge to combine actions with spiritual depth, implying that the practice of hospitality should not be detrimental to one's development of spirituality. To encourage readers to reflect on their own lives, such analysis asks them to consider the balance that they maintain between their spirituality and their service.

Martha, who is weighed down by her duties, requests that Jesus tell Mary to lend a hand with her. In response, Jesus says the words that are now famous: "Martha, Martha, you are worried and upset about many things, but few things are needed or indeed only one." Mary has made the better choice, and it will not be taken away from her (Luke 10:41-42). There has been a significant amount of interpretation surrounding this passage, with some people regarding it as a criticism of Martha's active service in favour of Mary's contemplative approach to service. On the other hand, a more in-depth analysis reveals a more complex comprehension of Martha's personality and the dynamic she shared with Jesus.

The tension between action and contemplation is exemplified in Martha's interaction with Mary, according to this example. In the Gospel of Luke, chapter 10, verse 39, it is stated that Mary sits at the feet of Jesus and engages with his teachings while Martha is busy with her duties. Martha's active involvement is contrasted with Mary's contemplative attitude to highlight the differing approaches to discipleship that are being highlighted. Jesus' response to Martha, "Martha, Martha, you are worried and upset about many things, but few things are needed or indeed only one" (Luke 10:41-42), invites Martha to re-evaluate her priorities. This moment can be understood as a summons to combine action with spiritual depth, implying that the practice of hospitality should not be detrimental to one's spiritual development. According to Brown (2003), this kind of analysis encourages readers to think about their own lives and the balance that they strike between their spiritual beliefs and their service to others.

Martha is frequently acknowledged for the part that she plays in serving Jesus, as described in Luke 10:38-42. According to Luke 10:40, she is shown to be "distracted by all the preparations that had to be made" when she invites Jesus into her house. In Jewish society, hospitality is a significant cultural value, and this passage serves as an example of her dedication to this practice. Martha's actions are a demonstration of her sense of duty and responsibility to provide for her guest, who is regarded as the Messiah. Through her service to Jesus, she exemplifies the spirit of hospitality that is essential to Jewish teachings, which hold that honouring the stranger is one of the most important things to do. On the other hand, her distraction is a sign that even the most dedicated servants can have difficulty with the challenges that come with their religious practice.

The scenario of Martha, the sister of Lazarus, in the Gospel of John (11:1-44) presents Martha in a different light than she is presented during the death and resurrection of her brother Lazarus. Once Jesus arrives in Bethany after the death of Lazarus, Martha goes out to greet him and engages in a meaningful theological conversation with him. In addition to expressing her conviction that Jesus was capable of healing Lazarus, she also reaffirms her faith in the resurrection. In response, Jesus makes the assertion, "I am the resurrection and the life." Even though they will die, the one who puts their faith in me will live; and the one who lives by putting their faith in me will never die. Do you have faith in this? Martha responds with a strong declaration of her faith, saying, "Yes, Lord, I believe that you are the Messiah, the Son of God, who is to come into the world" (John 11:27). Not simply a busy housekeeper, this conversation shows Martha to be a woman of profound religious conviction and theological comprehension.

Martha's character is ultimately one of deep faith, even though she was initially distracted by another person. In John 11:21-27, when she learns that her brother Lazarus has passed away, her first reaction is to convey her faith in the ability of Jesus to bring him back to life. Through her confession of faith, "I believe that you are

117

the Messiah, the Son of God" (John 11:27), the foundation of her ministry is a profound faith and grasp of who Jesus is. In addition to transcending her role as a server, this moment demonstrates the depth of her faith and serves as a challenge to believers to act out of faith when they are engaged in service. This multidimensional depiction of Martha offers a more nuanced understanding of her position within the biblical story, demonstrating that service and faith are interconnected concepts, with each one enhancing the other (Keller & Keller, 2013).

To comprehend Martha's actions and the reasons behind them, it is necessary to understand the historical and cultural context of her tale. In the context of first-century Jewish society, hospitality was considered a divine obligation, and women were predominantly responsible for administering the household and ensuring that guests were taken care of. This cultural norm is reflected in Martha's worry about ensuring that Jesus and his disciples are served a proper meal. Nevertheless, Jesus' answer calls into question the conventional gender roles and priorities that were in place at the time. Through his praise of Mary for her decision to listen to his teachings, Jesus places a higher emphasis on the significance of spiritual education and discipleship than on the obligations that come with being a household leader. It is not accurate to say that Jesus places less value on service or hospitality; rather, it is more accurate to say that he places a higher value on spiritual nourishment and attentiveness to his message. Over the course of Christian history, there have been different ways of understanding the narrative of Martha.

Using the contrast between Martha's active service and Mary's contemplative devotion, some commentators have sought to distinguish between the active and contemplative lives. This distinction serves as a foundation for their distinction. From this perspective, Martha symbolizes the practical and outward-oriented facet of faith, whereas Mary typifies the more spiritual and inward-oriented aspect of faith. In monastic traditions, where the balance between prayer and work is a central focus, this interpretation has been particularly influential since the balance between the two is a key concern.

Martha's character has been the subject of a more favourable evaluation by other interpreters, who have brought attention to her hospitality, diligence, and unwavering religion. They claim that Martha's service is an indispensable manifestation of her love for Jesus and that her deeds should not be dismissed as tasks. In addition, her pronouncement of faith in John 11 is evidence of her deep grasp of the mission and identity of Jesus. From this point of view, Martha's story serves as a reminder that faith is not only about meditation but also about actively engaging in the service of other people.

The story of Martha has been analysed by theologians and biblical scholars for its feminist aspects in more recent times. They contend that the depiction of Martha as a hectic, somewhat anxious woman reflects the social pressures and norms that were imposed on women during her time. Jesus empowers women to pursue their own spiritual development by challenging these norms and reaffirming Mary's entitlement to learn and grow in her spirituality. This reading brings to light the significance of Martha's narrative for current debates regarding gender equality and the position of women in the church.

The contemporary relevance of Martha's narrative stems from its capacity to address the difficulties and possibilities that come with living in today's world. Martha's example serves as a reminder to us that in a world that sometimes emphasizes output and success, it is essential to strike a balance between activity and contemplation and to discover meaning in the routine tasks that we do every day. In addition to motivating us to dig deeper into our own reasons for serving, her narrative also urges us to make sure that our actions are grounded in a sincere love for God and for other people.

In addition, Martha's narrative challenges the idea that there is just one "correct" way to convey one's religious beliefs. Both Martha and Mary provide valuable examples of discipleship, and the narratives of these two women imply that there is space for a variety of methods to faith within the Christian community. It is possible that some people are more interested in active service, while others are more interested in contemplative prayer and study. Both are vital components of a Christian living that is well-rounded.

It is anticipated that the understanding of Martha's narrative will continue to develop in the future as new generations of Christians wrestle with the challenges of faith and service in a world that is constantly changing. In a time when society is becoming more and more polarized and split, Martha's example of compassion and willingness to engage in conversation with Jesus may provide a template for fostering understanding and building bridges across differing points of view. Her tale serves as a reminder that, even while we are in the middle of our hectic lives, we may still find moments to connect with others, to listen to their stories, and to give them the gift of our presence.

To summarize, the narrative of Martha in the Bible is a rich and complex story that provides important lessons on the character of faith, service, and the balance that must be struck between reflection and action. In addition to being remembered for her active participation in the preparations for the household, Martha is also depicted as a woman of profound faith and theological comprehension. In addition to challenging conventional gender roles and priorities, her interactions with Jesus encourage us to consider the many ways in which we can show our love for God and for other people. By investigating the historical and cultural context of Martha's story, evaluating the influence that her story has had on Christian thought and practice, and exploring a variety of interpretations of her role in the story, we will be able to develop a deeper understanding of the intricacies of faith and the continuing significance that Martha's example holds for Christians today.

Martha's narrative provides significant insights into the essence of discipleship, particularly the critical role that active service imbued with spiritual awareness plays. Through her character, she encourages contemporary readers to reflect on their own lives and to discover a harmonious balance between acting and contemplating their spiritual interests. We learn from her example that hospitality is a profound demonstration of faith, and that discipleship entails a dynamic relationship between serving others and deepening one's connection to God.

# MARY OF BETHANY: A MULTIFACETED ROLE IN THE NEW TESTAMENT

Then Mary took about a pint of pure nard, an expensive perfume;
she poured it on Jesus' feet and wiped his feet with her hair. And
the house was filled with the fragrance of the perfume. (John 12:3)

Mary of Bethany is a person of great significance in the New
Testament. She is interwoven with major occurrences and
relationships that shed light on the character of Jesus and the
essence of faith. Mary of Bethany is also a figure who reveals the
nature of faith. In addition to featuring her with her sister Martha
and her brother Lazarus in the story of Lazarus's resurrection, the
Gospel of John specifically designates her as the lady who anointed
Jesus with perfume and wiped his feet with her hair. The purpose
of this chapter is to investigate the complex representation of
Mary of Bethany as it appears in the New Testament, with a focus
on her actions, the relationships she has, and the theological
ramifications that these actions and relationships carry. The chapter
will investigate the significance of her anointing of Jesus, her
participation in the resurrection of Lazarus, and the contrasting
yet complementary dynamics that exist between Mary and her
sister Martha. Through her deeds in these major stories, which
clearly reflect her personality and spirituality, this chapter contends
that Mary is a model of the virtues of devotion, faith, and the
transformative power of the presence of Christ.

The act of anointing Jesus by Mary of Bethany is the event that she is most well-known for, and it is described in the Gospels of Matthew, Mark, and John (Matthew 26:6–13; Mark 14:3–9; John 12:1–8). In the Gospel of John, the woman who does the anointing is named as Mary, the sister of Lazarus. This contrasts with the Gospels of Matthew and Mark, which do not identify the woman by name. In the Gospel of John, this anointing takes place at a supper that is taking place in Bethany six days before the Passover holiday. Mary takes a pound of expensive perfume that is composed of pure nard and pours it over the feet of Jesus, wiping them with her hair. The aroma permeates the entire house, and Judas Iscariot expresses his disapproval of the apparent waste, proposing that the perfume might have been sold and the proceeds donated to those who are less fortunate. In defence of Mary, Jesus argues that she has performed a lovely thing and that she has anointed his body in advance of the burial process.

There are numerous dimensions to the significance of Mary's anointing. To begin, it is an expression of deep love and dedication. The fact that Mary used expensive perfume reflects her willingness to present something that is of great value to Jesus, which is a demonstration of her deep love and respect for him. The anointing, in addition to its other meanings, has prophetic connotations. In his interpretation of Mary's act, Jesus emphasizes the imminent nature of his death by suggesting that she was anticipating his burial. This interpretation puts a greater emphasis on Mary's religious intuition as well as her comprehension of the purpose of Jesus. The anointing serves as a form of public recognition of Jesus' identity as the Messiah, which is the third point. In essence, Mary is anointing Jesus as king by anointing his feet, which is a way of acknowledging his divine authority and royal mission.

Mary's act of anointing Jesus with costly perfume is a demonstration of her profound devotion and recognition of the significance that Jesus held in her life. Mary is said to have taken a pound of pure nard and anointed the feet of Jesus, according to the record in John 12:3. This act was recorded in the Bible. Not only was this act one of physical care, but it also served as a manifestation of her understanding of the death that Jesus was about to experience and her commitment to pay tribute to him. There is an invitation to investigate the cultural and social standards of the time pertaining to presents to a rabbi (Borchert, 1996) when it comes to the lavish nature of the perfume, which was traditionally valued at a year's pay. In addition, the reply of Judas Iscariot, who chastised her for the extravagance, serves to accentuate the distinction between genuine devotion and misaligned priorities. It challenges readers to reflect on their own manifestations of faith.

When it comes to gaining a better understanding of Mary of Bethany, the narrative of the raising of Lazarus, which is recorded in John 11:1-44, offers yet another important perspective. When Lazarus becomes unwell, his sisters, Mary, and Martha, send word to Jesus, expressing their faith that he has the power to heal their brother. The arrival of Jesus is delayed, and Lazarus passes away. When Jesus finally shows up in Bethany, Martha goes out to meet him, while Mary remains at home. Mary is not there when Jesus arrives. In John 11:24, Martha conveys her trust in the power of Jesus to raise Lazarus by saying, "I know that he will rise again in the resurrection on the last day." In response, Jesus makes the assertive statement, "I am the resurrection and the life," which is recorded in John 11:25. He says that those who put their trust in him will live even if they die.

Following this conversation, Martha proceeds to Mary and informs her that Jesus has expressed a desire to meet with her. As soon as Mary arrives at Jesus, she throws herself at his feet and says, "Lord, if you had been here, my brother would not have died" (John 11:32).

Jesus is the first person she sees. In response to the sorrow that Mary and those who were with her were experiencing, Jesus inquires as to the location where Lazarus has been interred. He approaches the grave, instructs that the stone be taken away, and then he shouts, "Lazarus, come out!" (John 11:43) to the deceased person. In the scene where Lazarus comes out of the tomb, he is shown to be still bound by the linen wrappings that were used to bury him.

This moving statement reflects her conviction that Jesus is both a healer and a saviour. Additionally, Mary Mary's emotional reaction when Jesus arrives, together with her act of worship, serves to underscore the intensity of the bond that she shares with him. Not only does the raising of Lazarus act as a demonstration of Jesus' divine authority, but it also serves to reaffirm Mary's faith, as she experiences a miracle that is so powerful that it further cements her position as a disciple during a period of deep sorrow.

In the Gospel of John, the raising of Lazarus is a dramatic event that demonstrates Jesus' power over death and serves as a precursor to Jesus' own resurrection. Lazarus was raised from the dead. There are several different ways in which Mary's involvement in this story is important. She is in mourning and that she has faith in Jesus. Her act of falling at his feet is a symbol of submission and reverence. Mary's statement, "Lord, if you had been here, my brother would not have died," is an expression of profound trust in Jesus' capacity to heal, even though it also conveys a feeling of let-down and grief. The fact that she was there at the grave and that she witnessed the miracle of Lazarus being raised from the dead establishes her as a devoted disciple of Jesus.

There are many ways in which people can relate to Jesus, and the Gospels offer important insights into these different ways through the differing portrayals of Mary and Martha. Jesus is recorded as visiting the house of Mary and Martha in the book of Luke, chapter 10, verses 38 through 42. Mary, on the other hand, sits at the feet of Jesus and listens to his teaching, while Martha is concerned with serving Jesus and preparing for him. Martha grows upset and complains to Jesus, saying, "Lord, do you not care that my sister has left me to do all the work by myself? Tell her then to assist me." (Luke 10:40). Jesus replies to Martha, saying, "Martha, Martha, you are worried and distracted by many things; there is need of only one thing." Martha is concerned and anxious about many things. Mary is the one who has made the better choice, and this choice will not be taken away from her," (Luke 10:41–42).

Mary's importance goes beyond the individual experiences she had with Jesus; she is a symbol of the active involvement of women in the early Christian communities that existed before to today. Her devotion and profound grasp of the mission of Jesus are reflected in subsequent Christian stories that highlight the contributions that women have made to faith practices. According to academic, Mary is an archetypical figure of discipleship that challenges the frequently patriarchal story that was prevalent during that time. The texts encourage readers to appreciate the significant contributions that women make within the faith community by recognizing both Mary's reaction to Lazarus' death and her anointing of Jesus. This, in turn, alters the perception of leadership in the early Christian community.

The tension between active service and contemplative discipleship is highlighted in this episode. Although Martha's dedication to hospitality is admirable, Jesus argues that Mary's decision to pay attention to his teaching is of greater significance. Mary's position at the feet of Jesus is like that of a disciple who sits at the feet of a Rabbi, eager to learn from the Rabbi's knowledge and experience. A profound desire to comprehend Jesus' message and to develop in faith is reflected in her attentiveness to the words that he spoke with her. The emphasis that Jesus places on the significance of spiritual meditation and the necessity of putting one's relationship with him ahead of other worries is highlighted by his affirmation of Mary's decision.

It is not appropriate to interpret the differing representations of Mary and Martha as a rejection of the service that Martha rendered. Instead, they are intended to demonstrate how important balance is in the context of the Christian life. Discipleship is comprised of both service and contemplation, which are both vital components. Mary's attentiveness to Jesus' teaching serves as a model for spiritual development and comprehension, while Martha's hospitality and willingness to serve are both important contributions. Mary and Martha, when taken together, embody the complex character of faith and the various ways in which people can demonstrate their devotion to Jesus Christ.

Mary of Bethany has been the subject of theological reflection, artistic representation, and popular devotion over the course of several centuries. Her act of anointing Jesus has been interpreted in various ways, including as a representation of love, a symbol of sacrifice, and a sign of spiritual insight. It has been suggested that the rising of Lazarus was a demonstration of Jesus' authority over death and a foreshadowing of his own eventual coming back from the dead. The tensions that exist between the portrayals of Mary and Martha have been utilized to demonstrate the significance of both service and contemplation in the context of the Christian life.

According to the writings of the early Christian theologians, Mary of Bethany is commended for her modesty, devotion, and ability to discern spiritual matters. Augustine, for instance, emphasizes the importance of Mary's attentiveness to the teachings of Jesus as a paradigm for being a Christian disciple. In his teaching, he places a strong emphasis on the necessity of listening to God's word and permitting it to change one's life. In a similar vein, Gregory the Great highlights Mary's act of anointing Jesus as a model of selfless love and devotion to him. He invites Christians to follow Mary's example by dedicating their own gifts and skills to God, which is what he hopes they will do.

Mary of Bethany is frequently shown in the act of anointing Jesus' feet in works of art, with the scene serving as a symbolic depiction of love, humility, and devotion. Giotto, Titian, and Rembrandt are just a few of the artists who have portrayed the drama and emotion of this event, drawing attention to Mary's tender gesture and the fragrance that permeates the surrounding space. In these artistic depictions, Mary is frequently depicted as a woman of elegance and beauty, with her deeds expressing a profound sense of reverence and devotion to her faith.

Mary of Bethany is frequently called upon in instances of popular devotion to serve as a heavenly intercessor for individuals who are looking for comfort, healing, and spiritual guidance. Those who are in mourning, in anguish, or who are having difficulties with their faith find comfort and inspiration in her story. Mary serves as a model of love, humility, and devotion, which inspires Christians to cultivate a deeper relationship with Jesus and to have faith in his ability to heal and alter their lives.

It is anticipated that the study of Mary of Bethany will continue to develop in the future, with the emergence of new viewpoints and interpretations. It is possible that as scholars continue to investigate the historical, cultural, and social contexts of the Gospels, they will discover new perspectives on the activities and responsibilities of women in the early Christian community.

Furthermore, interdisciplinary methodologies that draw upon disciplines such as archaeology, sociology, and literary criticism have the potential to provide new insights into the representation of Mary of Bethany and the significance she holds for readers in the present day.

Mary of Bethany is a New Testament character who stands out as a significant figure because she embodies qualities such as love, devotion, and spiritual insight. There are numerous important insights that can be gained from her anointing of Jesus, her being present at the raising of Lazarus, and her being portrayed in a contrasting manner alongside her sister Martha. These lessons are about faith, service, and contemplation. Mary's narrative continues to inspire and challenge readers in the present day, encouraging them to deepen their relationship with Jesus and to embrace the complex dynamics that are involved in being a disciple. Her legacy continues to serve as a demonstration of the love's immense power, the humility's significance, and the faith's capacity to bring about transformation.

Devotion and faith are two important topics that may be learned from Mary of Bethany's actions in the New Testament stories, which provide profound insights. In addition to her anointing of Jesus, Mary also reflects unwavering discipleship and a profound comprehension of Christ's mission through her emotional journey surrounding the death of her brother Lazarus. In addition to serving as a significant narrative of individual faith, her depiction in the Gospels also reflects the broader role that women played in early Christianity. This challenges modern readers to consider the continuing effect that her story has had on faith practices in the present day.

# PRISCILLA AND AQUILA: THEIR ROLE IN THE EARLY CHURCH

He began to speak boldly in the synagogue. When Priscilla and Aquila heard him, they invited him to their home and explained to him the way of God more adequately. (Acts 18:26)

Through their evangelistic efforts, teaching, and acts of hospitality, Priscilla and Aquila, a Jewish couple who are referenced in the New Testament, made significant contributions to the establishment of the early Christian church. The rest of this chapter delves into the contributions they made, the theological significance they held, and the enduring influence they have had on Christian history and thought.

Their joint ministry with the Apostle Paul is a testament to their devotion to evangelism and education and demonstrates their commitment. The substantial contributions that Priscilla and Aquila made will be discussed in this chapter, with particular emphasis on the influence they had on the outreach initiatives of the early church to both Jews and Gentiles, as well as their mentoring of others such as Apollos. By looking into their collaborative ministry, we can see how they not only provided support to Paul in his evangelistic activities, but they also created a legacy that equipped future leaders and disseminated the message of Christ to a variety of cultures. This serves to demonstrate their pivotal role in the establishment of the early church.

Priscilla and Aquila are frequently acknowledged as a benchmark of collaboration in ministry, and they are said to successfully exemplify the principle of cooperative labour for the sake of the gospel. Both had the same profession of tentmaking and a love for evangelism, which provided them with a distinctive platform to connect with different communities around the world. When they first met Paul in Corinth (Acts 18:2), they welcomed him as a fellow worker and rapidly developed a close-knit partnership that was defined by common objectives and mutual support. Their ability to connect with both Jews and Gentiles, which has allowed them to expand the church's influence beyond cultural and ethnic boundaries, is evidence of the importance of their collaboration (Stott, 2020). The combined efforts of the two of them are an excellent illustration of how teamwork may enhance the effectiveness of ministry in local communities.

The narrative of Priscilla and Aquila is intertwined with the fabric of the early church, and it highlights important ideas such as partnership, hospitality, and commitment to the spread of the Gospel. Not only were they active participants in Paul's ministry, but they were also important leaders. They were not just figures who existed in the background.

Information regarding Priscilla and Aquila is primarily derived from the New Testament, particularly the Book of Acts and the letters that Paul wrote. After being expelled from Rome because to Claudius's order against the Jews, they eventually found themselves in Corinth, where Paul met them as described in Acts 18:1-3. This was probably around AD 49. Because they were all tentmakers by trade, they shared this vocation with Paul, which enabled them to work together and develop a strong relationship with one another.

From the city of Corinth, Priscilla and Aquila joined Paul's journey to Ephesus (Acts 18:18-19). After Paul went on with his trip, they stayed there to serve as ministers to the local community. Apollos was a skilled and knowledgeable speaker about the Scriptures, but he did not have a thorough understanding of the teachings of Jesus. They met him in Ephesus, where they were introduced to him. According to Acts 18:26, Priscilla and Aquila "took him aside and explained to him the way of God more adequately."

In several of his epistles, Paul expresses gratitude for the work of Priscilla and Aquila and recognizes the significance of these two individuals in the Christian community. He also expresses gratitude for their work. In Romans 16:3-5, Paul greets them and refers to them as "my fellow workers in Christ Jesus, who have risked their necks for my life." He expresses his gratitude to them, saying that not only is he grateful to them, but also all the churches of the Gentiles. Additionally, he says that the church in their home should be greeted. This verse demonstrates their devotion to Paul and their readiness to put themselves in danger for the sake of the Gospel. Not only that, but it also suggests that they had a house church, which was a widespread occurrence in the early church when Christians would come together for worship and fellowship in private homes.

In addition, 1 Corinthians 16:19 demonstrates their presence in Ephesus, as Paul sends greetings from "Aquila and Prisca, together with the church in their house." In 2 Timothy 4:19, which was written later in Paul's life, he sends greetings to "Prisca and Aquila" once more, indicating that they were in Rome at that time.

To have a better understanding of the significance of Priscilla and

Aquila's ministry, it is important to consider the historical context in which it occurred. The early Christian church was a movement that was both dynamic and expanding, and it encountered difficulties from both its own ranks and outside sources. It was necessary for Christians of many backgrounds, including Jews and Gentiles, to discover methods to coexist and worship together. In general, the Roman authorities were wary of new religious groups, and there was always the possibility of harassment. In this context, people such as Priscilla and Aquila played an important part in the expansion of the church, the dissemination of the Gospel, and the provision of safe places for believers to gather.

The fact that Priscilla's name is always mentioned together with Aquila's implies that they are involved in a ministry together. It was odd in that patriarchal culture for Priscilla's name to appear before Aquila's in certain instances, even though it did happen. Because of this, certain academics have arrived at the conclusion that Priscilla may have been the more gifted or renowned of the two individuals. Nevertheless, their marriage is a good example of a shared ministry model, in which both husband and wife work together to utilize their various gifts and abilities to serve God.

The narrative of Priscilla and Aquila teaching Apollos emphasizes their positions as teachers and mentors in the educational process. Although they saw Apollos's potential, they also acknowledged that he required additional teaching. In Acts 18:26, they were careful and gentle in their approach, as they "explained to him the way of God more sufficiently." In the context of the Christian life, this shows the significance of having a solid doctrine as well as the necessity of continuing discipleship.

Priscilla and Aquila were significant contributors to the propagation of the Gospel and the establishment of churches in several different cities. During the time that Paul was on his missionary journeys, they accompanied him, and, after that, they stayed in Ephesus to minister to the local community. A sense of community and support was fostered among the believers using their house as a meeting place.

The Priscilla and Aquila house church is an example of their hospitality and willingness to open their home to others. This fact highlights their kind attitude. During the time of the early church, house churches were essential for creating a safe and welcoming space for believers to worship, learn, and have fellowship together. The development of the Christian community was heavily influenced by the generosity of Priscilla and Aquila.

The narrative of Priscilla and Aquila has had a significant and long-lasting influence on the history and philosophy of Christianity, inspiring innumerable individuals to offer their gifts and abilities to serve God. Their model of partnership, teaching, evangelism, and hospitality continues to reverberate with Christians in the present day.

Priscilla and Aquila are excellent role models for Christian couples, as they exemplify the significance of shared ministry and the importance of supporting one another. Couples are inspired by their model to combine their talents to serve God and strengthen the church community.

Priscilla's story has been a great source of motivation for women who serve in the ministry. Having the position of a teacher and leader, she challenges the conventional views of women's roles within the church. Even though there are varying interpretations of specific passages of scripture that pertain to women serving in ministry, the example set by Priscilla provides a strong argument in favour of recognizing and affirming the talents and contributions of women to the church.

The house church of Priscilla and Aquila is a wonderful example of the significance of small groups and intimate settings for Christian community and discipleship. An important component of the Christian landscape, house churches offer a space for believers to connect with one another, study the Bible, and provide support for one another as they go through their various faith journeys.

When it comes to discipleship, the narrative of Priscilla and Aquila teaching Apollos offers several important insights. It emphasizes the significance of solid doctrine, the necessity of patient teaching, and the requirement for continual development in the life of a Christian. Through their example, Christians are encouraged to be both learners and teachers, constantly striving to deepen their understanding of God's Word and sharing it with others around them.

Priscilla was recognized for her significance by early church fathers like as John Chrysostom, who also commended the intelligence and bravery she demonstrated. Chrysostom emphasized the intellectual capabilities and spiritual insight of her subject, Apollos, and recognized her contribution to the teaching of Apollos.

Priscilla and Aquila made significant contributions to the church by mentoring and teaching important church leaders, which was one of their outstanding accomplishments. Apollos, a powerful speaker, and missionary who was initially ignorant of the entirety of Jesus' message, is a wonderful example of their interaction with him (Acts 18:24-26). Priscilla and Aquila, recognizing the potential that he possessed, extended an invitation to him to come into their house, where they instructed him and provided him with insights into the way of God in a more accurate manner. Not only did this act of mentorship serve to refine Apollos's rhetoric, but it also highlighted the significant role that the couple played in counselling leaders of the early church. Through their commitment to teaching, they demonstrate an empowering approach that stresses the importance of equitable involvement in ministry activities.

Priscilla's story has been brought to the attention of feminist theologians as a case study of a woman who demonstrated teaching and leadership talents within the early church. They contend that her example offers a foundation for affirming the roles of women in ministry and that it is a challenge to patriarchal readings of the Scripture.

The narrative of Priscilla and Aquila has been the subject of study by a considerable number of biblical scholars, who have investigated the historical context, the theological implications, and the connection that they had with Paul. Many important insights on their contributions to the early church have been provided by these academics.

Current authors are still writing about Priscilla and Aquila, investigating the relevance of these figures for the church in the present day. Their partnership, welcome, and commitment to spreading the Gospel are frequently emphasized as examples in these works.

There are many different opinions regarding the roles that Priscilla and Aquila played in the early church. Their collaboration with Paul is emphasized by certain academics, who consider them to be of assistance to his ministry and view them as such. There are those who emphasize the unique contributions that Priscilla made, asserting that she was a wonderful teacher and leader in her own other way.

The reading of 1 Timothy 2:12, which forbids women from teaching or having authority over men, is a source of contention among theologians and religious leaders. Several academics hold the view that this passage conflicts with the example set by Priscilla, while others believe that it is relevant to circumstances or contexts. Feminist theologians frequently analyse this section considering other passages of scripture that validate the talents and responsibilities of women in ministry. They argue that the example set by Priscilla presents a powerful counter-narrative.

The social and cultural context of the early church is the focus of another perspective. It was out of the ordinary for women to hold positions of leadership or authority in a society that valued male dominance. Priscilla's narrative challenges these standards, implying that the early Christian community was more receptive to the involvement of women than what certain conventional understandings would suggest.

A thorough biblical text, historical context, and a variety of theological viewpoints must be considered to properly analyse the narrative of Priscilla and Aquila. Even though interpretations may vary, the example that they set of partnership, teaching, evangelistic activity, and hospitality continues to be a significant and motivating model for Christians in the present day.

There were long-lasting consequences that resulted from the ministry of Priscilla and Aquila for the outreach efforts of the early church. As evidenced by their exile from Rome (Acts 18:2), their willingness to risk persecution is a testament to the steadfast devotion to their religion and the gospel message that they possess. In addition to the personal sacrifices that they made, they were instrumental in the formation of house churches, which served as the foundational gatherings for believers in several different cities (Piper & Taylor, 2007). These house churches were instrumental in the dissemination of Christianity during a period of social upheaval and opposition, which highlights their strategic importance in the development of the faith among both Jewish and Gentile converts respectively. As a result, their legacy continues to have an impact on present church activities that are centred on hospitality, community development, and leadership training.

There has been a resurgence of interest in the narrative of Priscilla and Aquila over the past several years, particularly in relation to discussions concerning women in ministry and the function of house churches. Priscilla's example has been used by some Christian groups and denominations to build a case for the acknowledgment and affirmation of women's talents and leadership. These groups and denominations have actively sought to promote this recognition and affirmation.

Priscilla and Aquila's approach to hospitality and community development has also received attention in several different parts of the world because of the proliferation of house churches and small group ministries. These movements reiterate the beliefs of the early church by highlighting the significance of close places for worship, discipleship, and mutual support.

It is anticipated that the narrative of Priscilla and Aquila will continue to serve as a source of motivation for Christians in the future, encouraging them to embrace partnership, exercise their gifts, and develop communities that are welcoming for believers. In the face of new problems and opportunities, the church may look to their example of commitment, bravery, and faithfulness as a source of inspiration.

Priscilla and Aquila were outstanding people who made important contributions to the establishment of the Christian church. The Gospel was disseminated, and the Christian community was strengthened because of their partnership, teaching, missionary work, and hospitality, all of which played a significant role. Their narrative continues to serve as an inspiration to Christians today, serving as a reminder of the significance of serving God and one another using our talents. Through the millions of people who have been inspired by their example of devotion, bravery, and love, their legacy continues to live on in the present day.

In the context of early Christian ministry, Priscilla and Aquila were two examples of a partnership that was both distinctive and impactful. Not only did their devotion to evangelism, teaching, and mentoring contribute to the spread of the gospel, but it also assisted in the development of a church community that is diverse and strong. By identifying and developing new leaders such as Apollos, they contributed to the successful and ongoing witness of Christianity across cultural divides. Their legacy is a powerful reminder of the significance of working together and having devotion to expand the church and advance its mission in the world.

# LYDIA OF THYATIRA: A PIONEER OF EARLY CHRISTIANITY IN EUROPE

When she and the members of her household were baptized, she invited us to her home. "If you consider me a believer in the Lord," she said, "come and stay at my house." And she persuaded us. (Acts 16:15)

Lydia of Thyatira is a significant person in the history of early Christianity, as she represents the spread of the Christian religion to Europe. The early church is discussed in this chapter, which examines her significance as the first European convert, her socio-economic status, her demonstration of Christian hospitality, and the influence she had on the early church.

The account of Lydia is found in the Book of Acts, specifically in Acts 16:11-15 and 40. This provides a window into the early days of the expansion of Christianity beyond its Jewish origins. In accordance with Acts 16:14, Lydia is presented in the story as a "seller of purple cloth, from the city of Thyatira, a worshiper of God." Her profession, place of origin, and religious proclivities are all revealed through this description, which provides insightful information about her background straight away.

The city of Thyatira, which is in modern-day Turkey, was well-known for its dyeing industry, especially to produce purple cloth. Fabrication of purple dye was a luxury item, as it was obtained from shellfish and used to colour clothes worn by royalty and high-class wealthy individuals. Given that Lydia was a seller of purple cloth, it is reasonable to assume that she was a prosperous entrepreneur who possessed both financial resources and social connections. The significance of this information lies in the fact that it refutes the prejudice that early Christians were made up entirely of those who were living in poverty and marginalized groups. The fact that Lydia became a Christian is evidence that Christianity was attractive to people from a variety of socio-economic backgrounds.

Lydia of Thyatira, who is mentioned in the New Testament as a dealer in purple cloth, is an important connection in the story of the early Christian church. As the first person in Europe to be officially documented as a convert to Christianity, her tale not only sheds light on her own faith journey but also on the larger influence that women had on the formation of early Christian communities. In addition, this chapter will assert that Lydia's significance in the spread of Christianity is demonstrated by her position as a businesswoman, her hospitality toward Paul and his companions, and her role as a leader in her community. Ultimately, Lydia's significance in the spread of Christianity challenges the gender norms of her day and recognizes the indispensable role that women played in the formation of early Christian communities.

In a society that is dominated by males, Lydia's identity as a collector and dealer in purple fabric highlights her financial self-sufficiency and her entrepreneurial spirit. In the ancient world, purple dye was considered a luxury item that was primarily connected with the upper class. This indicates that Lydia was not only a successful businesswoman but also a person of some affluence. A level of autonomy that was unusual for women of her era was made possible by her considerable financial resources. Through the course of her business, she would have found herself at the crossroads of trade networks connecting several cities, which would have resulted in an expansion of her influence and the formation of connections that would later assist in the spread of Christianity. One example of this is her ability to provide housing for Paul and the others, which is evidence of her prominent position and the resources she commanded within the social fabric of Thyatira. Lydia's achievement in business is not only a backdrop to her conversion; rather, it is a testimony to her position in society. It demonstrates that women were able to wield power and influence long before the complete establishment of Christianity.

It is likely that Lydia was a God-fearer, which is a term used to describe a Gentile who was interested in Judaism but had not completely converted to the faith. Her religious identity as a "worshiper of God" is indicative of this. Even though many Gentiles were drawn to the monotheism and moral teachings of Judaism, they were reluctant to embrace all the requirements of Jewish law, such as circumcision and dietary restrictions. Because there were God-fearers present, the Christian message was able to find an audience that was receptive. The message offered a route to faith in the God of Israel that was more accessible than others.

Lydia's life was forever altered with the arrival of Paul and his companions in the city of Philippi. Paul's missionary journey, which was directed by a vision (Acts 16:9-10), brought him to Macedonia, where he sought to spread the message of the gospel. Philippi, which was a Roman colony, was an important location for evangelism since it was the meeting point of Roman and Greek cultures.

In the book of Acts 16:14, it is said that Lydia's conversion was a direct result of God's intervention. It is written, "The Lord opened her heart to respond to Paul's message." The theological notion that conversion is primarily the work of God, rather than just a choice that is made by a human, is highlighted by this statement. Lydia's active participation in listening to and accepting the Gospel is also recognized, however, by this distinction. The fact that she was baptized later, together with her household, is a sign of a public assertion of her new religion and a commitment to continue following Christ. It is suggested by the baptism of her entire household that Lydia held a position of authority and influence within her family or business, and that her transformation had a ripple effect on those who were in her immediate vicinity (Witherington, 1998).

After Lydia had been baptized, she offered Paul and his companions the opportunity to come and stay at her house. She said to them, "If you regard me to be a believer in the Lord," (Acts 16:15) which means "come and stay at my house." There are multiple reasons why this demonstration of hospitality is considered essential. To begin, it is a demonstration of Lydia's devotion to Christian fellowship and her eagerness to lend her financial resources to support the work that Paul and his team are doing. According to Givens & Givens (2020), hospitality was an important component of early Christian faith. It served as a vital source of support for missionaries who were traveling and helped to develop a feeling of community among believers. In addition to being a place where believers could congregate and worship, Lydia's house became a centre for Christian activity in Philippi. It provided a haven for Paul and his companions.

After Lydia had been baptized, her first reaction was to ask Paul and the other people who were traveling with him to come and stay at her house. This response exemplifies the fundamental Christian value of hospitality. Not only is this act of devotion a matter of courtesy; rather, it reflects her solid commitment to the religion that she has recently adopted and her wish to assist Paul with his missionary efforts. Many times, the value of hospitality is highlighted in biblical narratives, and the actions of Lydia are consistent with this idea. It is implied that her house became a meeting place for the early Christian community in the city of Philippi. Through Lydia's willingness to welcome others into her home, the concept of women's involvement in the formation and nurturing of community is brought to light. This involvement also contributes to the maintenance of Christian beliefs. By accepting roles that are usually assigned to men and establishing herself as a key presence within the early church, Lydia not only aids in the spread of Christianity through her act of hospitality but also subverts the expectations that are placed on women during her time.

Lydia's hospitality, in addition to other factors, emphasizes her prominent position within the leadership of the early church. By extending an invitation to Paul and his team to make themselves at home in her house, she accepted the obligation of supplying their necessities and assisting their mission. Lydia was not just a convert, but also a leader who was instrumental in the formation of the Christian community in Philippi, as this implies. It is possible that other Christians would have been inspired to imitate her example of hospitality and service, which would have contributed to the expanding strength of the early church.

Not only does Lydia's conversion and hospitality have significance within the immediate context of Acts 16, but it also has significance beyond that.

Lydia, the first person in Europe to be baptized as a Christian, is a symbol of the spread of the Gospel to new places and cultures around the world. According to her narrative, Christianity was not restricted to a specific ethnic or social group; rather, it was available to anyone who were willing to put their faith in God. As a result of

Lydia's conversion, Christianity was able to spread further across Europe, which ultimately became a significant hub of Christian faith and influence (Johnson, 2011).

Additionally, Lydia's narrative offers important perspectives on the function that women played in the church during its early days. Even though women were frequently excluded from decision-making processes in ancient societies, the New Testament presents them as being actively involved in the Christian movement. In addition to providing hospitality, financial support, and leadership within the church, women such as Lydia, Priscilla, Phoebe, and Mary Magdalene were instrumental in assisting the ministry of Jesus and the apostles (MacDonald, 1996). Lydia's example defies traditional gender roles and demonstrates that women were vital contributors to the expansion and vitality of the early Christian community.

Lydia's impact is still being acknowledged and commended in present expressions of Christianity around the world. In several different Christian denominations, including the Roman Catholic Church and the Eastern Orthodox Church, she is honoured and remembered as a saint. There are a variety of dates on which her feast day is celebrated, which reflects the diversity of Christian liturgical calendars. Lydia's narrative is frequently used as an illustration of faith, hospitality, and leadership, which serves as a source of inspiration for Christians to adopt her values into their own lives (Hall, 1996).

The impact of Lydia extends beyond the specific actions that she takes; her conversion is a significant milestone in the development of Christianity in Europe and in the incorporation of women into the story that this movement tells. Her role challenges current notions of gender within the sphere of religion, urging us to reconsider the contributions that women have made to ecclesiastical history. In this context, women were not passive recipients of religious teachings but rather active participants and leaders, which reflects a broader trend that is being observed. Lydia's commitment to her religion and community is a legacy that would serve as an inspiration for future generations of women within the Christianity faith, reaffirming their invaluable contributions to the history of the church. As a result, Lydia's story not only enhances our understanding of the dynamics of early Christianity, but it also brings to light the continuing impact that women have had on the formation of religious communities.

There has been a resurgence of interest in recent years regarding the research of women mentioned in the Bible and the contributions they made to the founding of Christianity. To gain a more in-depth understanding of the roles that these women played and the significance that they had, scholars have investigated the historical and cultural contexts in which they lived. In addition to revealing the agency and influence of women like Lydia within the early church, this research has provided new insight into the lives of women.

In addition, Lydia's narrative has struck a chord with current debates around gender equality and the involvement of women in positions of power and leadership. Her portrayal of a successful businesswoman who employed her means to advocate for the Christian ministry challenges traditional views and offers a positive model for women who hold leadership positions. The narrative of Lydia serves as a reminder that women have always been an essential component of the church and that their contributions should be acknowledged and celebrated.

Lydia's story will continue to be a source of inspiration and challenge for Christians all around the world in the years to come. It is important to remember the life-changing influence of the Gospel and the significance of welcoming and supporting those who are new to the religion, as her model of faith, hospitality, and leadership serves as a reminder of both things. While the church continues to struggle with concerns relating to cultural diversity and gender equality, Lydia's narrative conveys a message of participation and empowerment that is relevant for all time.

In the history of early Christianity, Lydia of Thyatira is an outstanding representative. The hospitable support that she provided for the ministry of Paul and his co-workers was of vital importance. Her conversion was the first step in the spread of Christianity throughout Europe. Lydia, who was a successful businesswoman and a leader in the early church, challenges established stereotypes and exemplifies the important role that women played in the formation of the Christian faith. Her narrative continues to serve as a source of motivation and challenge for Christians today, serving as a reminder to them of the life-changing potential of the Gospel and the significance of including women in leadership positions and accepting diversity.

Her expertise in business is a demonstration of the possibility for women to exert influence and have autonomy in a society that is dominated by men. In addition, the manifestation of hospitality that she exhibited after baptism not only serves as a symbol of her devotion to her religion, but it also underscores the significant role that women played in the development of early Christian communities. As the first known person in Europe to convert to Christianity, Lydia's legacy serves as a powerful reminder of the important ways in which women have contributed to the church. It challenges modern readers to acknowledge and celebrate the diverse ways in which women have historically been involved in the areas of faith and community development.

# LOIS AND EUNICE: THEIR INFLUENTIAL LEGACY ON TIMOTHY'S FAITH

I am reminded of your sincere faith, which first lived in your grandmother Lois and in your mother Eunice and, I am persuaded, now lives in you also. (2 Timothy 1:5)

Timothy's grandmother and mother, Lois, and Eunice, respectively, are important persons in the New Testament. They are examples of how familial faith may have a powerful impact and how spiritual values can be passed down through successive generations. Considering the historical and cultural context of their lives, the theological ramifications of their devoutness, and the enduring impact that they have had on Christian education and discipleship, this chapter will explore the roles that they played in cultivating Timothy's faith and preparing him for his important ministry within the early Christian church. In biblical writings, the influence of mothers provides a strong narrative, as demonstrated by the influence of Lois and Eunice on Timothy's faith. Both women are dedicated and committed to the teachings of their respective religions, which has had a significant influence on Timothy's spiritual journey.

To grasp the importance of Lois and Eunice in Timothy's life, it is necessary to take into consideration the historical and cultural context in which they lived and ministered. They were women who practiced Judaism and lived in the city of Lystra, which was in the Roman province of Galatia. There were Jewish communities spread all over the Roman Empire during the first century, and they maintained their religious practices while also interacting with the Hellenistic culture that was around them (Goodman, 2006). When it came to the practice of Judaism, this atmosphere offered both difficulties and opportunities. These communities, on the other hand, were exposed to the widespread influence of Greek philosophy, Roman governance, and the religious rituals of polytheistic faiths. In contrast, the diaspora provided an opportunity for the spread of Jewish beliefs and values to a larger audience, which laid the groundwork for the subsequent expansion of Christianity (Hayes, 1999).

Although the New Testament contains few biographical facts about Lois and Eunice, their religion is prominently mentioned in 2 Timothy 1:5, where Paul writes to Timothy, "I am reminded of your sincere faith, which first lived in your grandmother Lois and in your mother Eunice and, I am persuaded, is now in you" (New International Version). According to this paragraph, both women played a significant part in helping Timothy develop a faith that was both real and unflinching. A faith that is real, sincere, and profoundly established in their lives is what the term "sincere faith" is meant to convey.

Timothy's mother, Eunice, and Lois, who was Timothy's grandmother, were both women of the Jewish faith who played a significant role in the development of Timothy's faith when he was very young. According to the scriptural allusions made in 2 Timothy 1:5, Lois and Eunice are shown as having a genuine faith that is free from doubt, which implies that they are both dedicated to a life of worship and adhere to Jewish traditions. As an illustration, one can see Eunice's influence in her choice to teach Timothy about the Scriptures, which was a practice that was not often seen among women during her period. Not only did this one-of-a-kind approach provide Timothy with theological knowledge, but it also equipped him with a moral framework that would enable him to confront the challenges that he would face in his ministry. Nurturing a child's faith can have enduring effects on their future, as evidenced by the influence that these women have had on their children. This emphasizes the essential importance of familial faith, which is a topic that runs all through the New Testament.

It is impossible to overstate the impact that Lois and Eunice had on the spiritual development of Timothy. According to Laffey (1988), traditional Jewish education placed a significant focus on the involvement of women in the religious formation of young people. In the home, women were primarily responsible for teaching children the fundamental tenets of Judaism, even though formal religious instruction in the synagogue was usually reserved for men. According to Neyrey (1990), this consisted of teaching in the Torah, prayer, and the observance of certain religious traditions and festivals.

Timothy's own ministerial journey was influenced by the actions of Lois and Eunice, which served as a model for him. Both Lois and Eunice exemplified practical faith through their actions. Not only was their dedication to the principles of God and teachings intellectual; rather, it was reflected in their daily lives. The illustration of courage and tenacity that is required for successful faith transmission is provided by Eunice's decision to rear Timothy in a Hellenistic society that frequently conflicted with Jewish values. Timothy is described in Acts 16:1-3 as having a good reputation among the believers, and this reflects the fact that he was taught by his grandmother and mother. This is an accomplishment that can be directly ascribed to the foundational teachings that his mother and grandmother imparted to him. In addition, the fact that Timothy ultimately worked alongside Paul in spreading the message of the gospel serves to illustrate the ways in which Lois and Eunice equipped Timothy to adjust his faith to engage with a variety of cultures.

During Timothy's early childhood, Lois, who is the grandmother, probably played a significant part in exposing him to the teachings of the Jewish scriptures and the traditions of the Jewish faith. Grandparents frequently play a special role within the household, as they are responsible for imparting knowledge, offering guidance, and creating a sense of continuity with the history. It would have been possible for her devoutness to serve as a living example for Timothy, illustrating the significance of faith in one's everyday life. In her capacity as Timothy's mother, Eunice would have been responsible for continuing this religious education, which involved nurturing his grasp of the scriptures and assisting him in applying the lessons he learned from them to his own life. It is probable that Eunice encountered difficulties in bringing up Timothy in the Jewish faith since she was married to a Greek man, as stated in Acts 16:1. In addition to demonstrating her own devotion, her commitment to doing so demonstrates her determination to impart her religious culture to her son.

It is possible that Eunice was required to deal with the challenges of interfaith marriage while also making certain that Timothy was given a solid foundation in the beliefs and practices of Judaism. To do this, she would have needed both courage and conviction, as she tried to maintain her religious identity within a family that may not have shared her dedication to the same extent. It is a credit to Eunice's effectiveness in conveying the value and significance of her religious practices that Timothy accepted the faith that his mother held and embraced it.

Considering the transmission of faith and the involvement of women in religious education, the devoutness of Lois and Eunice has major theological repercussions. This is especially true about the relationship between faith and women. Their example serves as a demonstration of the significance of intergenerational faith, providing an example of how intentional teaching and personal role modelling can be used to transfer religious beliefs and values from one generation to the next (Clinton & Stanley, 1992). Their narrative brings to light the significant impact that women have in cultivating the faith of their children and grandchildren, a role that is frequently undervalued or ignored in religious environments that are based on conventional practices.

In addition, the faith of Lois and Eunice challenges the idea that religious leadership and influence are exclusively the province of men. Even though they may not have had official positions of authority within the early church or the synagogue, Timothy's spiritual development was significantly influenced by their presence, which equipped him for a lifetime of service and ministry. Through the roles that they play as mothers, grandmothers, teachers, and mentors, women can have great spiritual influence, as evidenced by their narrative. They can shape the lives of those around them and to contribute to the development and well-being of the faith community.

In addition to imparting knowledge of the scriptures, Timothy's preparation for ministry involved several other components as well. It also involved teaching him how to pray, encouraging him to build a personal connection with God, and instilling in him a desire to serve others, in addition to modelling a life of faith. It is possible to learn these components of spiritual formation most effectively when they are taught within the context of a loving and supportive family environment.

Timothy was a faithful friend and co-worker of the Apostle Paul, and he played an important part in the preaching of the gospel and the founding of the early church. In addition to preaching, teaching, and planting new churches, he assisted Paul during several missionary travels (Fee, 2013). Timothy was given significant duties by Paul, such as the leadership of congregations, the resolution of disputes, and the appointment of church leaders. There were difficulties that occurred during Timothy's administration. In addition to the internal disputes that he dealt with within the congregations that he ministered to; he was confronted with opposition from those who rejected the gospel. Despite this, he kept his devotion to Christ and his mission, relying on the Bible and the guidance of the Holy Spirit to help him through the challenges that he was experiencing.

The two letters that Paul sent to Timothy, which are preserved in the New Testament, offer significant implications for Timothy's character and the work that he did. In these letters, Paul exhorts Timothy to be faithful to the teachings that he has received, to be on the lookout for false doctrines, and to continue to be faithful even when he is confronted with challenges. In addition, Paul stresses the significance of being a person of honesty, humility, and love, and he sets an example for others to emulate.

The outstanding legacy that Lois and Eunice left behind is demonstrated by the influence that Timothy had on the early church as well as the continuing impact that the letters Paul wrote to Timothy have had on the church. Their narrative continues to serve as a source of inspiration for Christians today, serving as a reminder to them of the significance of family faith, the contribution that women make to religious education, and the strength that encompasses all generations of discipleship.

Lois and Eunice's narrative is still very pertinent today, and it provides important insights for families, churches, and educational institutions. It is impossible to overstate the significance of passing on one's faith and values from one generation to the next in an era characterized by the rise of secularism and the emergence of moral relativism. Parents and grandparents have a distinctive opportunity to instil in children a love for God, a knowledge of the scriptures, and a commitment to living a life that is both purposeful and meaningful. Families play an important part in the spiritual and moral development of children.

In addition, churches can take inspiration from the examples set by Lois and Eunice by fostering cultures that assist and promote relationships that span multiple generations. It is possible to close the gap between various age groups and develop a sense of community and belonging using intergenerational worship services, family ministries, and mentoring programs. As a means of allowing younger people to learn from the faith and resilience of their elders, these projects offer opportunities for older adults to share their knowledge and experience with younger generations.

Additionally, the narrative of Lois and Eunice emphasizes the significance of empowering women in positions of leadership and religious education initiatives. It is essential that women be acknowledged and celebrated for the significant impact they have on the formation of the spiritual lives of their children, grandchildren, and communities through their contributions. For women to be able to minister using the gifts and talents that God has given them, churches and other faith-based organizations should provide them with opportunities and supply them with the resources and support that they require to be successful.

There are also important lessons that can be learned from the difficulties that Eunice encountered while bringing up Timothy in the Jewish faith, despite being married to a man of Greek descent, for interfaith families today. There is a growing trend toward interfaith marriage in many regions of the world, and these families frequently find themselves confronted with difficulties when it comes to navigating their religious identities and bringing up their children in a manner that respects both of their faith traditions. To establish a family atmosphere that is harmonious and supportive, the case of Eunice underscores the need of open communication, mutual respect, and a willingness to compromise.

Both Lois and Eunice had a significant impact on Timothy that went beyond the specific interactions they had with him; this influence created a legacy that continues to reverberate throughout Christian teachings. They provide an opportunity for reflection on the functions that mentorship and spiritual guidance play within the faith community. They emphasize that the presence of female figures in the biblical story has a significant impact that is sometimes not recognized. Therefore, the early preparation of Timothy by his mother and grandmother is not just a personal experience, but rather a communal legacy that emphasizes the necessity of nurturing faith among families in the present day. This endeavour also reinforces the significance of women's roles in the formation of spiritual leaders.

Timothy's faith was profoundly influenced by Lois and Eunice, who also prepared him for the important part he would play in the early Christian church. For Christians in the present day, their devoutness, commitment to religious education, and intergenerational impact provide a strong role model to follow. They serve as a reminder to us of the significance of family faith, the part that women play in the religious education process, and the everlasting impact that intergenerational discipleship has. By following their example, families, churches, and educational institutions can contribute to the development of the faith of future generations and prepare them to make a transformative impact on the world.

The dedication that Lois and Eunice must nurturing Timothy's faith is a wonderful testimony to the profound influence that family may have on the formation of a person's spirituality. Their example serves to demonstrate the significance of maternal characters in biblical stories, as well as the lasting impact that these figures leave behind through their faith and the encouraging messages that they impart. Not only did Timothy acquire knowledge and develop character because of the nurturing atmosphere that Lois and Eunice created, but he also launched an important ministry that connected the early church with the various community that it served. This story continues to have an impact on contemporary debates regarding the role of families and communities in spiritual upbringing, reminding us of the enduring significance that these foundational connections have.

# BIBLIOGRAPHY

Ackerman, S. (1998). Warrior, Dancer, Seductress, Queen. New Haven: Yale University Press.

Alter, R. (2008). Five Books of Moses: A Translation with Commentary. London: W W Norton & Co Ltd.

Alter, R. (2011). The Art of Biblical Narrative. New York: Basic Books.

Aquinas, T. (1274). Summa Theologiae.

Armstrong, K. (2007). The Great Transformation: The Beginning of our Religious Traditions. New York: Anchor.

Barton, J. (1986). Oracles of God. London: Darton Longman and Todd.

Barton, J. (2002). The Biblical World. Oxford: Taylor & Francis.

Barton, J. and Muddiman, J. (2007). The Oxford Bible Commentary. Oxford: Oxford University Press.

Berlin, A. (2005). Poetics and Interpretation of Biblical Narrative. Winona Lake: Eisenbrauns Printing.
Berlin, A., Brettler, M.Z. and Jewish Publication Society (2014). The Jewish Study Bible. Oxford: Oxford University Press.

Blenkinsopp, J. (2009). Judaism, The First Phase: The Place of Ezra and Nehemiah in the Origins of Judaism. Grand Rapids: William B.

Eerdmans Pub. Co.

Blenkinsopp, J. (2015). Abraham: The Story of a Life. Grand Rapids: William B. Eerdmans Publishing Company.

Bock, D.L. (1994). Luke. Downers Grove: Inter-Varsity Press.

Borchert, G.L. (1996). John. Nashville: Broadman & Holman.

Brenner, A. (1995). A Feminist Companion to Esther, Judith and Susanna. Sheffield: Sheffield Academic Press.

Brenner, A. (1997). The Intercourse of Knowledge: On Gendering Desire and 'Sexuality' in the Hebrew Bible. New York: Brill.

Brenner, A. (2014). The Israelite Woman. London: Bloomsbury Publishing.

Bright, J. (2000). A History of Israel. Louisville: Westminster John Knox Press.

Brock, R.N. and Thistlethwaite, S.B. (1996). Casting Stones. Minneapolis: Augsburg Fortress Publishing.

Brown, D. (2003a). The Da Vinci Code. New York: Delacorte Press.
Brown, P. (2013). Augustine of Hippo: A biography. Berkeley: University Of California Press.
Brown, R. (2003b). An Introduction to the Gospel of John. Yale: Anchor Bible.

Brown, R.E. (2016). Introduction to the New Testament. New Haven: Yale University Press.

Brueggemann, W. (2008). Old Testament Theology: An Introduction. Abingdon: Abingdon Press.

Campolo, T. (2005). Speaking My Mind. Nashville: Thomas Nelson.

Carson, D.A. (1999). Jesus' Sermon on the Mount: And His Confrontation with the World: An Exposition of Matthew 5-10. Grand Rapids: Baker Books.

Catholic Church (2019). Catechism of the Catholic Church. Liguori: Liguori Publications.

Collins, J.J. (2018). Introduction to the Hebrew Bible, Third Edition: The Writings. Minneapolis: Augsburg Fortress Publishers.

Dever, W.G. (2002). What Did the Biblical Writers Know and When Did They Know it?: What Archaeology Can Tell Us about the Reality of Ancient Israel. Grand Rapids: William B. Eerdmans Publishing Company.

Dunn, J.D.G., Rogerson, J.W. and Day, J. (2003). Eerdmans Commentary on the Bible. Grand Rapids: William B. Eerdmans Publishing Company.

Ehrman, B.D. (2012). Forged: Writing in the Name of God- Why the Bible's Authors Are Not Who We Think They Are. New York: HarperOne.

Evans, C.A. (2013). Jesus and His World: The Archaeological Evidence. Louisville: Westminster John Knox Press.

Exum, C. (1992). Tragedy and Biblical Narrative Arrows of the Almighty. Cambridge: Cambridge University Press.

Fee, G.D. (2013). Pauline Christology: An exegetical-theological study. Grand Rapids: Baker Book House.

Fox, M.V. (2010). Character and Ideology in the Book of Esther. Eugene: Wipf & Stock.

Fretheim, T.E. (1996). The Pentateuch. Abingdon: Abingdon Press.

Friedman, R.E. (2019). Who Wrote the Bible? New York: Simon & Schuster Audio.

Frymer-Kensky, T. (1992). In the Wake of the Goddesses. New York: The Free Press.

Frymer-Kensky, T. (2002). Reading the Women of the Bible. New York: Random House Inc.

Gafney, W. (2017). Womanist Midrash: A Reintroduction to the Women of the Torah and the Throne. Louisville: Westminster John Knox Press.

Gaventa, B.G. (1999). Mary: Glimpses of the Mother of Jesus. Minneapolis: Fortress Press.

Givens, F. and Givens, T. (2020). All Things New: Rethinking Sin, Salvation, and Everything in Between. Meridian: Faith Matters Publishing.
Goodman, M. (2006). Judaism in the Roman World. Leiden: Brill.

Green, J.B. (1997). The Gospel of Luke. Grand Rapids: William B. Eerdmans Publishing Company.

Hall, D.J. (1996). Professing the Faith. Minneapolis: Fortress Press.

Hall, J. (1983). A History of Ideas and Images in Italian Art. London: John Murray Publishers.

Hayes, J.H. (1999). Dictionary of Biblical Interpretation. Nashville: Abingdon Press.

Hays, R.B. (1996). The Moral Vision of the New Testament: Community, Cross, New Creation:A Contemporary Introduction to

New Testament Ethics. San Francisco: Harper.

Holy Bible. (2004). New Revised Standard Version ed. Oxford: Oxford University Press.

Horsley, R.A. (2003). Jesus and Empire. Minneapolis: Fortress Press.

Johnson, L.T. (2009). Among the Gentiles. New Haven: Yale University Press.

Keener, C.S. (2014). The IVP Bible Background Commentary: New Testament. Second ed. Downers Grove: Intervarsity Press.

Keller, T. and Keller, K. (2013). The Meaning of Marriage: Facing the Complexities of Commitment with the Wisdom of God. London: Hodder & Stoughton.
Kenyon, K.M. and Morley, P.R.S. (1987). The Bible and Recent Archaeology. Atlanta: John Knox Press.

King, K.L. (2003). The Gospel of Mary of Magdala: Jesus and the First Woman Apostle. Santa Rosa: Polebridge Press.

Kugel, J.L. (2001). The Bible as it Was. Cambridge, Mass.: The Belknap Press Of Harvard University Press.

Laffey, A.L. (1988). An Introduction to the Old Testament: A Feminist Perspective. Minneapolis: Fortress Press.

Landy, F. (2010). Paradoxes of Paradise: Identity and Difference in the Song of Songs. Sheffield: Sheffield Phoenix Press.

Lane, T. (2007). A Concise History of Christian Thought. London: T & T Clark.

Levenson, J.D. (1995). Death and Resurrection of the Beloved Son : Transformation of Child Sacrifice in Judaism and Christianity. New

Haven: Yale University Press.

Levenson, J.D. (2015). The Love of God: Divine Gift, Human Gratitude, and Mutual Faithfulness in Judaism. Princeton: Princeton University Press.

Levine, A.J. and Knight, D. (2011). The Meaning of the Bible: What the Jewish Scriptures and Christian Old Testament Can Teach Us. New York: HarperOne.

Luke Timothy Johnson and Harrington, D.J. (2006). The Gospel of Luke. Collegeville: Liturgical Press.

MacDonald, M.Y. (1996). Early Christian Women and Pagan Opinion: The Power of the Hysterical Woman. Cambridge: Cambridge University Press.

Mazar, A., Stern, E., Meyers, E.M. and Chancey, M.A. (1990). Archaeology of the Land of the Bible. New York: Doubleday.

Meyer, M.W. and De Boer, E. (2004). The Gospels of Mary: The Secret Tradition of Mary Magdalene, The Companion of Jesus. San Francisco: Harper San Francisco.

Meyers, C.L (1991). Discovering Eve. Oxford: Oxford University Press.

Meyers, C.L (2013). Rediscovering Eve: Ancient Israelite Women in Context. Oxford: Oxford University Press.

Meyers, C.L., Arnold, B.T. and Witherington, B. (2005). Exodus: New Cambridge Bible commentary. Cambridge: Cambridge University Press.

Miller, J.M. and Hayes, J.H. (2008). A History of Ancient Israel and Judah. Louisville: Westminster John Knox Press.

Milton, J. (1667). Paradise Lost. London: Penguin Classics.

Neyrey, J.H. (1990). Paul, in Other Words. Louiseville: Westminster John Knox Press.

Northouse, P.G. (2021). Leadership: Theory and Practice. 9th ed. Los Angeles: Sage Publications.

Pagels, E.H. and King, K.L. (2008). Reading Judas: The Gospel of Judas and the Shaping of Christianity. London: Penguin Books.

Piper, J. and Taylor, J. (2007). The Supremacy of Christ in a Postmodern World. Wheaton: Crossway Books.

Plaut, G. and Stein, D. (2015). The Torah: A Modern Commentary. New York: Reform Judaism Publications.

Rahner, K. (1964). Mary, Mother of the Lord. Spring Valley: Crossroad Publishing.

Raymond Edward Brown (1999). The Birth of the Messiah. New Haven: Anchor Yale Bible Reference Library.

Sarna, N.M. (1995). Understanding Genesis. New York: Schocken Books.

Schaberg, J. (2004). The Resurrection of Mary Magdalene: Legends, Apocrypha and the Christian Testament. London: Continuum.

Schäfer, P. (2009). Jesus in the Talmud. Princeton: Princeton University Press.

Schüssler Fiorenza, E. (1992). But She Said: Feminist Practices of Biblical Interpretation. Boston: Beacon Press.

S.D Parks (2005). Leadership Can Be Taught: A Bold Approach For a

Complex World. Boston: Harvard Business School Press.

Smith, M.S. and Miller, P.D. (2012). The Early History of God: Yahweh and the Other Deities in Ancient Israel. Grand Rapids: William B. Eerdmans Publishing Company.

Stanley, P.D. and Clinton, J.R. (1992). Connecting: The Mentoring Relationships You Need to Succeed in Life. Colorado Springs: Navpress.

Stanton, E. (1972). The Woman's Bible. Alexandria: Library of Alexandria.

Stein, R.H. (1992). Luke. Nashville: B & H Publishing Group.

Stott, J. (2020). Message of Acts. St Louis: Intervarsity Press.

Trible, P. (1978). God and the Rhetoric of Sexuality. London: S.C.M.

Trible, P. (2022). Texts of Terror (40th Anniversary Edition): Literary-Feminist Readings of Biblical Narratives. St Louis: Fortress Press.

Walton, J.H. (2011). Genesis 1 as Ancient Cosmology. Winona Lake, Ind.: Eisenbrauns.

Warner, M. (2016). Alone of All Her Sex: The Myth and the Cult of the Virgin Mary. Oxford: Oxford University Press.

Webb, B.G. (2012). The Book of Judges. Grand Rapids: William B. Eerdmans Publishing Company.

Williamson, H.G.M. (1985). Ezra, Nehemiah: 16 (Word Biblical Commentary). Waco: Word Books.
Wills, G. (2011). Augustine's Confessions : A Biography. Princeton: Princeton University Press.

Witherington III, B. (1997). The Jesus Quest: The Third Search For the Jew of Nazareth. Downers Grove: Intervarsity Press.

Witherington III, B. (1998). The Acts of the Apostles: A Socio-Rhetorical Commentary. Grand Rapids: Eerdmans.

Witherington III, B. (2001). Women in the Ministry of Jesus: A Study of Jesus' Attitudes to Women and Their Roles as Reflected in His Earthly Life. Cambridge: Cambridge University Press.

Witherington III, B. (2007). The Letters to Philemon, the Colossians, and the Ephesians: A Socio-Rhetorical Commentary on the Captivity Epistles. Grand Rapids: Eerdmans.

Wright, N.T. (2012). After You Believe: Why Christian Character Matters. New York: Harper Collins.

Wright, N.T. (2015). Jesus and the Victory of God. London: Society for Promoting Christian Knowledge.

Zornberg, A. (2011). The Particulars of Rapture: Reflections on Exodus. New York: Schocken Books.